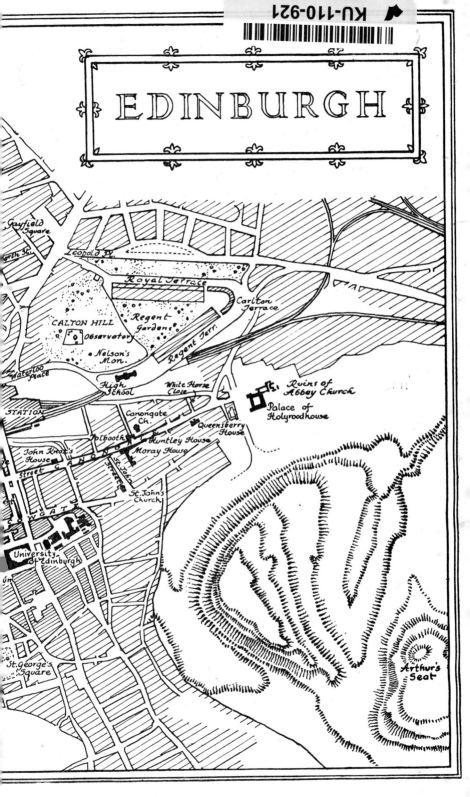

EDINBURGH

Gayfield
Square

rth St.

Leopold Pl.

Royal Terrace

CALTON HILL

Regent
Gardens

Carlton
Terrace

Observatory

Nelson's
Mon.

Regent Terr.

Waterloo
Place

High
School

White Horse
Close

Ruins of
Abbey Church

STATION

Canongate
Ch.

Palace of
Holyroodhouse

Tolbooth

Queensberry
House

John Knox's
House

Huntley House

Moray House

Street

St. John

COWGATE

St. John's
Church

University
of Edinburgh

St. George's
Square

Arthur's
Seat

EDINBURGH

1 Edinburgh Castle from the Grassmarket

From a lithograph by
W. L. Leitch

EDINBURGH

By

GEORGE SCOTT-MONCRIEFF

*With 114 Illustrations from Engravings,
Paintings and Photographs*

LONDON
B. T. BATSFORD LTD.
15 NORTH AUDLEY STREET, W.1

Dedicated to the memory of
my Wife and my Brothers,
with whom I shared
my Edinburgh days.

Ann Scott-Moncrieff, 1914–1943
Colin Herbert Scott-Moncrieff, 1908–1941
Charles James Scott-Moncrieff, 1919–1942

Requiescant in Pace

First Published, Spring 1947

MADE AND PRINTED IN GREAT BRITAIN
FOR THE PUBLISHERS, B. T. BATSFORD LTD., LONDON
BY MORRISON AND GIBB LTD., TANFIELD, EDINBURGH

INTRODUCTION

WHILE I WAS WRITING THE ENSUING PAGES THERE CAME THE news of the atomic bomb, making curious inroads into one's consideration of one's own ploys. I thought how very academic my book could become. There was, suddenly, a chance that copies of it might survive its subject, which had naturally seemed inevitably more permanent than any comment I might make upon it. Even accounts of what has happened to some of the German towns suggests that a city of long-standing, rich in history and fine buildings, may by modern methods be immediately reduced to mute rubble. It is a disconcerting thought : cities like Edinburgh seem so permanent that we grow fiercely indignant over the pointless destruction of a few fine buildings at the hands of old-fashioned philistines.

However, I hope that this will not become an academic study, but serve, like one of the caddies of the old days, to introduce my native city to the interested visitor.

Even within the limits of my own knowledge there are many deserving incidents, places and personalities that have received inadequate comment or sometimes no comment at all. I have found it difficult to leave out so much that I have enjoyed and wanted to discourse upon. As it is, there are considerable digressions that would ill-become a formal guide-book. I hope, however, that these lend perspective to the views of Edinburgh that I have selected : and that the total effect gains more than it loses through being observed from an individual viewpoint.

Particularly, I have dealt rather briefly with the contemporary scene. But here one is always up against insoluble difficulties of selection : a wealth of material which if fully exploited would obscure the bigger picture with often insignificant minutiæ.

In hoping that I have not been unfair in certain statements, I feel I must make it plain that none of my passing references to St. Andrew's House reflect upon the many estimable and conscientious persons amongst its inmates. They relate only to a tendency of which we are fellow-victims, and they the worse sufferers, towards that bureaucratic existence that as we have seen, however well-meaning its inception, must either at last topple upon reaching the limit of human ability to effect controls in a free country, or flout freedom and civilisation by enforcing itself with Gestapo or N.K.V.D. I am sure that the present personnel of St. Andrew's House regards this latter alternative with as much horror as do I. We only differ in our assessment of the gravity of the present threat to national and individual freedom and dignity.

*   *   *   *   *   *   *

I am indebted to the works of many predecessors : particularly I should like to mention some studies on the New Town written by John Summerson, A.R.I.B.A. I have had much kindly help from private individuals : notably Sir Frank Mears, P.R.S.A., Dr. Meikle, late of the National Library, and Dr. Malcolm in the graceful setting of the Signet Library. Mr. Butchard and Miss Balfour of the Edinburgh Room in the Central Library were most helpful in providing my publishers and myself with selections of engravings for illustration. Mr. R. Aitken, bookseller in Bruntsfield, kindly lent a portfolio of prints in his possession. I owe many other persons, not least old friends amongst the Edinburgh booksellers, my thanks and appreciation.

GEORGE SCOTT-MONCRIEFF.

HEBRIDES,
January 1947.

CONTENTS

ACKNOWLEDGMENT

THE Publishers have pleasure in acknowledging their obligation to the following sources for the prints and photographs which illustrate this book : Robert M. Adam, for Figs. 2, 3, 12, 15, 19, 22, 24, 31, 38, 40, 43, 56, 58, 61, 69, 83, 91, 94, 105, 106, 108, 109 and 112 : R. Aitken, Bookseller, Edinburgh, for Figs. 23, 38 and 73 ; J. C. H. Balmain, for Figs. 59, 62, 103 and 104 ; Miss Violet Banks, A.R.P.S., for Figs. 9, 18, 57, 71, 85, 96, 98 and 107 ; The Central Library, Edinburgh, for Figs. 7, 8, 20, 21, 26, 27, 30, 51, 54 and 72 ; The late Brian C. Clayton, for Figs. 32, 33, 37, 52, 53 and 74–77 ; David Octavius Hill, for Figs. 11, 65, 66, 92 and 93 ; Messrs. Hislop & Day, Edinburgh, for Fig. 39 ; Messrs. Judges, Hastings, for Fig. 25 ; The London, Midland & Scottish Railway (Publicity Department), for Fig. 5 ; Donald McLeish, for Figs. 10 and 70 ; E. H. C. Moffat, for Figs. 88, 99 and 100 ; A. Reiach, for Figs. 36, 60, 89, 110, 113 and 114 ; *The Scotsman*, for Figs. 6, 13, 87, 90, 95, 101 and 102 ; George Scott-Moncrieff, for Figs. 34, 35, 84, 86 and 111 ; Messrs. Valentine & Co., for Figs. 16 and 78. The remainder of the subjects are from originals in the possession of the Author and of the Publishers. The endpaper map of present-day Edinburgh has been specially drawn for the book by Miss Norah Davenport.

2 Canongate Tolbooth

3   The Castle, looking across the Grassmarket from the Vennel

The Castle

I

IT IS THE WAY OF GREAT CITIES TO STRADDLE A RIVER. Even after the navigable importance of the river has diminished with the swelling tonnage of shipping, it remains a symbol dear to the citizen ; the riverside a place for young men to ponder the mutability of existence, or, crossed in love, pleasantly to contemplate suicide. Even the roaring traffic of to-day seems less significant of the city's flow and life stream than does the drumlie ooze of its river, winding between streets and houses, below bridges, terraces and blackened embankments. Edinburgh's river is the Water of Leith ; so small a stream, even at its best, viewed from the impressive height of the Dean Bridge, you would hardly think that it could sustain a capital city or the imagination of her young men. Moreover, it runs only through the New Town and the less tidy housing that link it with the Port of Leith, nowhere does it impinge upon the original City along its snell ridge from Castle to Canongate.

Edinburgh is in that respect unusual ; her shape has never been affected by the flow of water. Her very name signifies a slope. She grew, in the Scottish manner, out of a single street ; a high and windy street on the crest of a ridge. Where most cities seek shelter in a valley, drain the water-meadows, sternly guide the river flow, and inhale the damps of ghostly marshes, Old Edinburgh rode high, sib to the winds, in harsh and drastic exposure.

St. Margaret's Chapel, on the Castle Rock, is the oldest building in Edinburgh. With its building, by the Queen Saint, about the year 1090, conjecture, fable and conceit, Roman urns and references to ancient forts, give place to history tolerably well chronicled, and tangible in the four walls of the chapel.

Queen Margaret, of the English reigning house, brought up in Hungary, married to the noble king, Malcolm Canmore, has been accused of weakening the native Celtic culture by her introduction of Continental ideas and civilisation into Church and State. But

A   1

the accusation cannot seriously be sustained. Queen Margaret's reforms were necessary to the maturity of the nation, and they were achieved in the best way humanly possible. The way, in fact, of a saint. She brought no invading army to ram *kultur* down the thrapples of savages, noble or otherwise. She set up no Gestapo or Departments of Light and Culture. She came to a position of leadership, as consort and beloved wife of the King, and assumed it with becoming modesty. What she brought was nothing contrary nor exotic, but the continuing growing rich fruit of western European civilisation. Scotland was already a well-defined Christian State. Her religion was not so much corrupt as ingrown, from the isolation consequent upon warfare. Queen Margaret opened the doors again to universal thought without harrying unduly those of her adopted nation who were to give it that flavour of the particular that turns thought from abstraction to an active element in the lives of men.

Malcolm and Margaret did not establish Edinburgh as their Capital, which remained across the Forth, at Dunfermline. That was left to the following reign, that of their son, David I. Yet Margaret's Chapel has every claim to be the foundation stone of Edinburgh ; or, like a minute cornucopia, we may see it as overflowing the Castle rock, down the ridge to the east, forming a lovely jewel at Holyrood, and flowing on, a life-stream through the centuries, at first limited by the bounds of the Old Town, but in the eighteenth century spreading rapidly across the lower land to the north. In the nineteenth century the flow became still quicker, although there was some decline in the quality of workmanship that housed the new life. By the present century the flow has become somewhat giddy, and we a little apprehensive that it may be going too far and too fast.

Architecturally, little enough has been of a standard with the mother building. Although so small—measuring only twenty-six feet by ten—it has instant beauty. It has been given a curiously perched appearance, through the cutting away of the rock for a roadway in the sixteenth century. At the same time, this emphasises its position, on the very summit of the Castle rock— the highest as well as the oldest foundation in the City—reemphasising that Edinburgh is a city of the heights, of the hill rather than of the valley, cold and hardy. The original masonry is typical Norman work—dressed rectangular blocks of freestone. Above and below it there is later work of rubble.

Within the square walls it is rather surprising to find a semi-circular, stone-vaulted apse. The vault of the nave, and other details, are alterations of about a hundred years ago. The arch separating nave from apse is Norman work, probably of the reign of Margaret's son.

Despite alterations, St. Margaret's Chapel remains authentically itself. A cell, a casket of stone ; with that graceful Norman quality, restrained and contemplative, unlike the inspired meditation of Gothic but with perhaps a purer sense of devotion. No city could ask a meeter primal building.

It has withstood all the vicissitudes of siege and storming that the Castle has suffered. When, in 1313, Randolph, Earl of Moray, Bruce's nephew, recaptured the Castle from the English by climbing the rock and delivering a surprise assault, he levelled, at the King's command, every building and fortification except the Chapel. After the Reformation, the Chapel became the Gunners' Storehouse, and a reformed chapel was built against the east wall. But in the last century it was once again treated with some respect, although not used for regular worship. And now we may enter it for an outlay of sixpence.

Across what was once the Governor's garden, to the south of St. Margaret's Chapel, and a cobbled roadway, there stood at one time another church, St. Mary's. It formed one side of the Palace Yard, and its site is now occupied by the National War Memorial (5).

There has been some unjust criticism of the Memorial, but it has suffered worse from paeans of uncritical praise. No doubt it is hard on the Memorial to visit it immediately after being in the Chapel. The one is self-conscious : the other has the obliviousness of the purposeful, certain and timeless. Indeed, it is necessary, if we are to be just, to see the Memorial in relation to its time— the 1920s, the Great Uneasy Peace. It was not a period of certitude in anything except that it was certainly self-conscious. What of the Memorial ? The masonry is excellent, and pays tribute to that most splendid tradition of Scottish stone masons, perhaps, in its persistence, the greatest in the world—for it continued from the tenth century right up to our own day : and even the worst of Victorian architectural freaks was customarily carried out with the same magnificent craftsmanship. In itself, the masonry does serve as a national commemoration : for the men who died were of the stock that long maintained the fine heritage of conscientious building.

The architecture is not so satisfactory. Sir Robert Lorimer was a fine architect, with a number of beautiful buildings to his credit. To discern why the Memorial does not rank with the best of these we are bound to consider its nature. What exactly is it ? It is not a chapel. It is not even an entrance hall or a gallery, it leads nowhere. One need not be a perfervid mediævalist to be convinced that a building must have purpose, a function, if it is to have form. Indeed, it is doubtful if at any other period of our history so inherently pointless a building could have been put up. Were it a chapel there would be an altar (or at least a pulpit) to provide a focus, and the whole construction would have been shaped to a definite, well-defined, and immediately comprehensible end. Even a library or a picture gallery would have imposed that proper limitation upon form that is essential to inspiration. In the apsidal projection the living rock appears through the floor, not architectonic but, again, self-conscious. The generation that has lost its menfolk might find, casting into memory, some suggestiveness in the Memorial: to subsequent generations its essentially unsatisfying nature must make it rather a curiosity. Yet, it is a memorial to a puzzled age: it has its place.

II

Across the Palace yard, otherwise known as The Close, from the War Memorial is the Great Hall built by James IV at the beginning of the sixteenth century. It is a museum now, with suits of armour ranged against a wooden Gothick screen, but has a fine old roof with carved masks of men and beasts at the ends of the hammer-beams. The stone supporting corbels are also carved. They are in that Renaissance manner of curiously barbaric civilisedness to be seen at its best in Scotland in the figures on James's Palace at Stirling. It is a manner very suggestive of his reign, with its culture at once robust and stylish, bursting with a native force, informed by classical learning. One of the corbels bears the head of a man against a leafy background that is supposed to be the King himself, and another shows the bust of a woman, supposedly his Queen, Margaret Tudor. But the height of the roof makes the detail difficult of appreciation.

Underneath the Hall are the Casemates, vast vaulted chambers used as prisons even to the time of the Napoleonic wars. Their doors bear still the names of Dutchmen and Frenchmen and rough carved pictures of ships and gallows. The vaults run under part of the Queen Anne buildings that occupy the west side of the Palace square. These were barracks built at the time of the Union, now used as a military museum. They present an unassuming but douce and pleasant face to the Close.

The fourth, the east side of the Close, is occupied by the Palace

4   The Palace Close.   *From a print of* 1829

5   The 1914–19 National War Memorial, in the Palace Close

6   The National Gallery, the Mound, and the Castle

itself. As Royal Palaces go it is not one of the most impressive, for the Castle early became of secondary importance to the other Edinburgh home of the kings, the Palace of Holyroodhouse. Yet it owes much of its present appearance to James VI, for it was remodelled and heightened in honour of his return visit to Scotland in 1617. When the king left his native country for London and the Throne of England in 1603, one of the Scottish noblemen gave offence by coming to bid him farewell dressed in full mourning. He excused himself with dignity, saying that England's gaining a king was Scotland's loss of one. It is easy nowadays to under-rate what indeed it did mean to Scotland to lose the presence of her King with the life and leading of the Court. In fact it was bound rather to play into the hands of a certain joyless element focussed in the Kirk—which had already tried conclusions with James, and been worsted. In those days at least, only puritans could be pleased at the loss of the display and pageantry that went with kingship.

Another misfortune of the absentee kingship from which Scotland suffered so long is the dispersal, pillaging and destruction of so much of the furnishings of her Royal Palaces. Customarily they were converted into barracks at one time or another, which allowed little chance for the survival of any refinements. The Palace at Stirling was shockingly treated. That at Linlithgow, the grandest of them all, was gutted by Hanoverian troops stationed there in 1746 : a few pieces of furniture from it survive in private collections as testimony to what it contained. The King's Lodging in Edinburgh Castle retains only one chair of all the furnishings that made it once sumptuous and regal. Panelling and moulded plaster ceilings have disappeared. The graceless Oliver Cromwell erased the Royal Arms and Monograms that embellished the exterior. These were carved for James's visit by the King's Master Mason, one William Wallace, a justly famous carver of his day, other of whose vigorous work may still be seen on the Palace walls.

Over £25,000 Scots was spent in refurbishing the Royal apart-ments for the King's return, and there were terrific entertain-ments, fireworks, music, pageantry and dancing, which may have distressed the puritans but must have been a great delight to the commonalty. He was a strange character, scarcely-lovable, but shrewd, and he provided good excuse for the human need, then somewhat starved in Scotland, for junketing and indulgence.

He had started his earthly existence in that same building. And the room of his birth is comparatively intact to this day.

B   5

After St. Margaret's Chapel, it is the most moving, the most personal and intimate, part of the Castle. It is very small. Its window looks out, over the Esplanade and the long street of the Old Town towards Holyrood, over the reek and the stour to the blue sky above what was then open country. Here on a summer day, in agony of soul and mind as great as the agony of her body, Mary bore Darnley's son. By her heroic fight to preserve the life of the baby whom her noblemen would have murdered in the womb, Mary is the only ruler in the Europe of her day whose descendants retain their crown. The line of kings was perpetuated. Mary's personal tragedy and that of her country moved on behind the public jubilation. The jubilation is commemorated on painted wooden panels of wall and ceiling : with Royal Crowned Mono-grams, M. R. and J. R., and the date, 19th June 1566, the Royal Stewart coat of arms and a verse. The tragedy has its own commemoration, and Mary of Scots survives to typify tragic queenship and womanhood, calling forth reproach and admiration, fealty and antagonism, from generations who never saw her and poets who never knew her country.

Problems represented as irreconcilable in the lives of such people as Mary have a quaint way of promoting the most palpable fictions, as though these would simplify, by reducing to more familiar proportions, inscrutable facts. Early in the nineteenth century, in a hole in the palace wall that was probably a beam-socket, some workmen discovered a rag, a fragment of bone, and some rotted wood—presumably a pickle of rubbish and the remains of the beam itself. Very quickly the wood was imagined into a coffin, the rag became cloth-of-gold embroidered with royal initials, and the bone was identified as that of a newly born infant. Further conjecture established the result as the entombment of Mary's real son, and James VI was declared a changeling. Apart from all else, the possibility of the survival for centuries of the bones of a newly born infant was never questioned ! Probably the legend will persist as meet fodder for trivial minds despite any attempt to dislodge it.

III

Just as the Castle is in every way the emblem of Edinburgh, constantly appearing and reappearing above the roofs and the streets of the City, so all Edinburgh unfolds itself to the observer from the Castle walls (7). On a clear day a fair swatch of Scotland itself may be seen. From the parapet in front of the Chapel, that

7 View from the Castle, 1824. *From a lithograph by J. Gendall*

8 The Castle with the New Barracks seen from the Grassmarket
From a print of c. 1830

9   The ramparts in winter, looking to the Tolbooth spire and St. Giles's

cumbrous lady, Mons Meg, sticks her dumb and harmless muzzle in the direction of the Firth of Forth, one of the many slashes of sea that strike into the body of Scotland. In the sunshine, houses and towns and villages glow against the green of the Fife coast, with a splash of red on the aluminium ore lying by Burntisland, and the hills of Fife break into the sky : the Cleish Hills, the Lomonds, and to the west the high plateau of the Ochils. These are Lowland hills, but beyond them, fifty miles from the Castle Rock, can be seen outposts of the Highland mountains : Ben Vorlich and Stuc a Chroin. This is looking well into the heart of Scotland, beyond Stirling, that ancient royal city that boasts a palace and a castle rock even finer and more shapely than Edinburgh's. Ben and Stuc are Perthshire heights, above " lone Glenartney " and " bonnie Strathyre " and girding Loch Earn.

From the big eighteenth-century, New Town style, barrack block, the view south-west runs along the Pentland Hills, the nearest of which, Allermuir, brings a grouse moor within the City bounds, to the fuggy air that hangs over Clydeside and the once flourishing, now declining, industry of the West. From the Half Moon bastion, built on the remains of the great tower of David II, if there is a wind to clear the reek from the lums and breweries of the Canongate, we are rather surprised to find ourselves looking out to sea, for the coast takes a southern slant just east of the City.

Land and history come close to mind from the vantage of Edinburgh Castle. And the City's own history is intimately wrapped with that of the Citadel. Randolph, Earl of Moray, and his men were led up the Castle Rock for their surprise assault by a certain William Francis, who took them up a secret path he had learnt " when I was young and somewhat volagious : " *i.e.* voluptuous. For in his youth as a member of the Castle garrison, Master Francis had found a way down the rock to enable him to pay nightly visits to a lady friend in the Town. Then there was that unfortunate Borderer, one Pringle, who in 1715 carelessly displayed a rosary in an ale-house in the High Street and betrayed a similar promising plot to surprise the Castle garrison. A handsome lass, Rob Roy's granddaughter, came from the City dressed as an aged cobbler with a pair of re-soled shoes for her father, James Mhor MacGregor, two days before he was to be hanged, deftly changed clothes with him and brought off one of the few escapes from the Castle. He had been condemned for assisting his brother in the abduction of a wealthy young widow, and, veteran of the '45, he lived in France until the Revolution : but his young brother swung in the Grassmarket for a crime scantily proved.

Most remarkable is the manner in which the Honours of Scotland survived all kind of revolt, including the fate of the English Crown Jewels under Cromwell, and finally returned to the light of day after over a hundred years of disappearance.

The Honours, now displayed in their case in the Crown Room, consist of the crown, the sceptre, and the sword of state. The origin of the existing crown is uncertain, but it was remodelled for James V in 1540. Either then or earlier the two bands of the coronet were embellished with two hoops to contain the royal velvet. On the whole this grandiosity is a decadence in a crown, reducing it to the style of a hat. However, it may gain a certain emphatic magnificence, perhaps consonant with a decadence in kingship. Diamonds, pearls, both oriental and native Scots, topazes, amethysts, carbuncles, are the jewels, and the coronet is decorated with fleurs-de-lys and crosses. The sword of state was a gift from Pope Julius II sent to James IV in 1507, with its scabbard a fine piece of Italian workmanship. The sceptre was also a papal gift, made to James by Alexander VI in 1494 : but, like the crown, it was remodelled by his son. There were of course many other jewels amongst the Honours : jewels and baubs bought and gifted, sold, lost and stolen at various times. Queen Mary brought with her from France the Great Harry, a famous diamond that her son took to England, where it was set in the Mirror of Great Britain, but disappeared at the Cromwell dispersal. It was in Mary's reign that that noble soldier, Kirkaldy of Grange, held the Honours in the Castle and refused to give them to the King's Party to crown her son. So that for the Parliament held at Stirling in 1571 it was necessary to make dummies of silver—the Queen's Party said they were brass—double-gilded, in order that the Honours might be formally represented.

Charles I wished the Honours to be sent to England for his Coronation, but was compelled to come to Holyrood to be crowned King of Scotland. In the Civil Wars the Honours were for a time hidden in Dalkeith, but were surrendered when the Castle was given up to the Presbyterians in 1640. Thereafter followed their strangest adventure. Taken to Dunnottar Castle on its seabound rock on the Angus coast, besieged by the Cromwellians, they were smuggled out of the Castle by Christian Fletcher, the wife of James Granger, minister of Kineff. The minister buried them under the floor of the kirk, where they lay hidden until the Restoration. " Cannonnes were lowsit and dischargit " at the triumphal return of the Honours to the Castle in May 1662.

At the time of the Act of Union there was much anxiety in Scotland lest the Honours were to go, after all, to England. It was necessary to include a special clause in the Act, by which they " are never more to be used, but kept constantly in the Castle of Edinburgh." The Earl Marischal, their keeper, refused to attend the degrading ceremony at which they were locked away. Thereafter, they came to be forgotten. But a dark suspicion lingered, and grew, that after all they had been taken south. Permission was eventually obtained from George IV to enter the Crown Room and force the locks of the great oak chest. Sir Walter Scott, apprehensive lest " a national affront and injury had been sustained," was one of those present when the Honours were rediscovered.

With the crown, the sceptre, and the sword, was found a rod of silver surmounted by rock crystal that is somehow supposed to have been the Lord High Treasurer's mace, but may equally have been the sceptre of some queen of the fifteenth century. The last surviving official post in connection with the Lord High Treasurer in Scotland is the King's Remembrancer, in whose custodianship the Honours remain. They include now some later Stewart relics, the Great George and Collar of the Garter, the St. Andrew of the Order of the Thistle, and a ring reputed to have been worn by Charles I at his coronation. These were bequeathed to George III by Henry, Cardinal of York, last of that extraordinary and ill-fated line, of which Voltaire declared that if anything would make him believe in fate, it was the history of the Royal House of Stewart.

IV

To the shopping parade of Princes Street the Castle brings the spectacular. It rides on its rock like a full-rigged ship poised on the crest of a majestic wave, about to plunge into the trough of Lothian Road (1). The green gardens forenenst it are in summer dotted with people in a lively genre. The flowers up the steep banks can make a gay blaze : and the scent of wallflowers welling over the pavement above is a delight. The floral clock by the garden steps at the foot of the Mound is always an extraordinary attraction : telling more wasted time than any, with its group of studious admirers hanging on the balustrade, watching the herb-filled hands slowly ticking round. Each year some new ingenious motif is devolved by the City's gardeners and pricked

out in little plants. Marvell anticipated the feelings of those many
who linger at the foot of the Mound to watch :

> How well the skilful gardener drew
> Of flowers and herbs this dial new !
> Where, from above, the milder sun
> Does through a fragrant zodiac run :
> And, as it works, th'industrious bee
> Computes its time as well as we.
> How could such sweet and wholesome hours
> Be reckon'd, but with herbs and flowers !

Those who protested at the floodlighting of the Castle surely
misinterpreted its quality. Its glory is scarcely architectural, for
its buildings are a medley of good, bad, and indifferent. Yet their
sum is effective, not excluding the contribution of the often-
maligned, cliff-like New Barracks : their setting on the rock is
splendid : and the situation of the whole, in the middle of the
mixter-maxter of a modern city, has a grand fantasy to it.
Certainly they are happier in the variety of more subtle daylights
and twilights, in dreamy sunlight, or snow-tipped in rose-pink
sunset, than under the glare of electric lamps. But floodlighting,
bringing them out of darkness into being, makes its own rather
stagey, or even filmic, interpretation. Floodlit, the buildings look
less those of a castle than those of a floating romantic city conjured
out of the gap of blackness : curiously cold and remote from the
clatter and clack of the pavements of Princes Street, yet signal-
ising that this is no place other than Edinburgh, Capital, leader,
and reprobate.

Inside the Castle to-day the greatest liveliness left is in the
School of Piping, high up in the Palace rooms. Here, under the
Piobaireachd Society, the doyen of military pipers, Pipe-Major
Ross, teaches the intricacies of fingering the Great Music, and
inspires his pupils with his artistry. Before the late war almost
every pipe-major in the regular army took the courses. During
the war short courses were given to hundreds of pipers, Scots and
Dominion, and even to a pipe band with which a Polish regiment
equipped itself.

It was a great sight, the young men from the Highlands and
farther places, each achieving his ambition in qualifying for the
course, fingering his chanter and wheepling those strangely moving
mountain airs under William Ross, himself a contemporary
version of those many Highlanders who have made Edinburgh
their home and figured in vignettes of the City's history. A big
man, like the vast figure of Grant of Burnside, seen in 1745
chasing, single-handed, a party of hussars through the streets

10

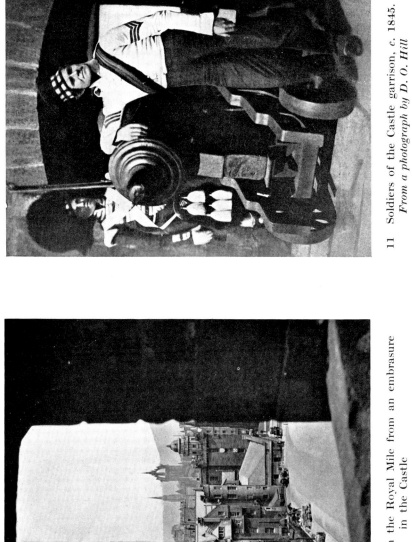

11 Soldiers of the Castle garrison, c. 1845. *From a photograph by D. O. Hill*

10 Looking down the Royal Mile from an embrasure in the Castle

12 The Castle above the City, from the Royal Botanical Garden

to the Castle gates : and when the fighting was over, Grant of Burnside became a respected W.S. in the City. The streets lie beyond the Palace windows on all sides now, tumbling north to the Forth : beyond and westwards the mountains echo the music with their rise and fall. The slightly dead, museumesque atmosphere that lies about so much of the Castle, is dissipated by the sound of the living music, with its strong happiness or poignant recollection of battles long ago, expressing immemorial emotions in an ancient vernacular.

Holyrood

The Church—The Abbey—The Palace—Shadows—John Knox—
Mary Stewart—The Abbey Precincts

I

HOLYROOD LIES AT THE FOOT OF THE BRAE, THE FAR END OF the Royal Mile : like a stone flung from the Castle to set the limits of the old community : the first fine gem to fall from St. Margaret's casket on the Castle height. The legend of the Abbey's foundation is of Margaret's son, David I, breaking a holy day by hunting, saved from death on the antlers of a stag, and building the Abbey on the spot in penance. An antlered stag, with the cross on its forehead, is the coat of arms of the Burgh of the Canongate, and presumably fathered the legend, for it was Queen Margaret's cross of ebony and ivory and silver that gave the name to Holyrood.

Some Augustinian Canons were first installed in the Castle. About the time that he founded their Abbey at Holyrood, David also founded the City itself : giving his knights and retainers parcels of land on each side of the brae. The colony expanded until it reached half a mile from the Castle, and later the other half of the Royal Mile was constituted as a separate burgh under the Canons of Holyrood ; the Canongait, *i.e.* way, walk, or road, whose first burgesses were the artisans, French, Flemish, and Scots, who for fifty years were building the conventual range beneath the crags and the height of Arthur's Seat.

It is difficult now really to comprehend what Holyrood Abbey was. The Palace sits above and somewhat dwarfs the sad relic of the church (13). Founds in the cut grass behind may map the outlines of the vanished buildings, but it is a dead ploy. To see the walls grow from them you would need to be a genius of a rare sort, with consummate knowledge that nevertheless had not overlaid the imagination with academic preoccupation. And even then it can only be a dream. Scottish history is bisected by an uncommonly ideological Reformation and the oppression generated of the triumph of English bad-neighbourliness. It is even hard for us to understand what precisely happened in the sixteenth century : the kind of theoretic puritanism that descended heavily upon so much that was rich and coloured and delightful, and yet on account of some persisting native fervour, never filled the whole picture. Then again, what are the strands that run through, each side of the gulf, back and fore ? Certainly, our Reformation was far more drastic than England's. Far less of the mediæval flowering was carried over to bloom afresh in post-Reformation Scotland. In its place came an astonishingly rank growth of philistinism. Externally, it has little beauty, but beneath it, like periwinkles beneath dusty evergreens, there were flowers.

We have to accept these ruins as they are, and only look back at what they were as to history that has served its time, leaving its indelible, if only dimly comprehensible mark. Only the roof-less nave of the Abbey church stands : two splendid Norman doorways lead from daylight to daylight and blind interlaced arcading binds the stripped stonework. One only of the two square Norman towers remains, the other was demolished to make room for extensions to the Palace.

Like most of the pre-Reformation Scottish churches, the fabric of the church at Holyrood actually suffered less from the zeal of the Reformers than from its lack. It was the neglect that was the common lot of kirks after the sixteenth century that brought the Abbey church by slow degrees to its present state of crumbled ruin. Before then of course it had suffered various depredations from English invasion : notably in 1544 when Hertford plundered and pillaged all the abbeys in the south of Scotland. The brass eagle lectern stolen by one of Hertford's knights on that occasion is still in the possession of the church at St. Albans to which he presented it. Even more, the fate of Holyrood, and of much else, was sealed by James V granting, with papal approval, the abbacy to his seven-year-old bastard, Robert Stewart : (he provided such sinecures for five of his bastards in all). This Commendator of Holyrood was outstanding amongst the crop of rakehellies who seized the opportunity of the collapse of order, as then somewhat tenuously held by the Church in Scotland, and, under the style of " Reformer," made frantic hay in the ensuing disorder. He used some of the Abbey stones to build himself a home, the Commendator's House, right in front of the west entrance to the Abbey. But in 1569 he sought pastures new, going to Orkney technically to see that the kirks there might be put in order, he forced Adam Bothwell to swap his bishopric and holdings in the Orkneys and Shetlands for the abbacy and perquisites of Holyrood.

Adam Bothwell was as impious, but of a meaner mould. Under him the Abbey church fell into graver decay. It was he who conducted in the Palace picture gallery (then the Hall), the grim nuptials forced upon Queen Mary by the Earl of Bothwell, and who later was the Queen's harshest accuser at Northampton. He was buried under the imposing and strictly untruthful epitaph in the Abbey church. And his son, as first and last Lord Holyroodhouse, inherited the monastery and much of its property.

Hertford's burning of the Abbey buildings and partial defacement of the church, had been duly followed, in 1567, immediately after the imprisonment of Mary, by the smashing of all the statues and altars by a vicious fanatic, the Earl of Glencairn. The Commendator had avoided responsibility for repairing the damage by cutting off the choir and transepts, reducing the church to its present framework. Charles II ultimately ordered the removal of the remains of choir and cross kirk that they might not clutter the environs of his Palace : his father was responsible for the present big mullioned east window. Presumably under James VI the truncated nave had been put into tolerable repair, for he married Anne of Denmark there. After a further period of neglect it was repaired for the coronation of Charles I (although Scone of course was the traditional place of coronation for the Scottish kings). That was a gay glint in a drumlie age : the church lit with tapestries and canopies of silk and velvet, the Lords present and the Lyon King at Arms : and outside the rabble crowding for the flung largesse, while those suffering from scrofula had their heads touched by the King.

Thereafter, it served as parish kirk for the Canongate until in 1688 James VII converted it into a Chapel Royal with an altar once again, and with stalls for his revived Knights of the Thistle. This last glory of the church was destroyed by the mob on the news of the Prince of Orange arriving in London. The witless fanatical hands broke into the Royal vault and smashed the coffins. From then until the early nineteenth century the Abbey church of Holyrood was left a filthy ruin, a monstrous object of neglect. An eighteenth century effort to put on a roof was so cumbrously done that it collapsed, with further damage. Darnley's skull and the embalmed head of the beautiful Madeleine, daughter of the French king and first wife of James V, were amongst the trophies stolen. Hugo Arnot, in his History of Edinburgh of 1776, gives a mordant description of walking amongst the litter of Royal remains.

To-day the Church stands one of those monuments to inter-

13 Holyrood, looking towards Arthur's Seat

14 The interior of the Palace quadrangle, as carried out by Sir William Bruce for Charles II

15 The Abbey of Holyrood

rupted decay in which Scotland is so sadly rich. We seem to cherish them because of an unhappy, and unhappily justified, doubt that we can build anything of comparable merit. It is certainly a healthier attitude than that more arrogant one which a hundred years ago prompted the refacing in improved nineteenth century Gothick of St. Giles's Church. And may we be saved to-day from a ridiculous suggestion that the Abbey Kirk be re-roofed as a " Valhalla " memorial to the dead of the second world war. Better to leave it now, tribute both to past creativeness and past destructiveness, than to flaunt our present barrenness by dolling its remaining sorrowful grace into any such meaningless confection.

II

Between 1178, when the Augustinian Canons walked the Royal Mile to take up their residence in the Abbey of Holyrood, and Hertford's depredations in 1544, there were many periods of peace and plenty. Sometimes, perhaps, rather much plenty for piety. From Great Paxton in Leicestershire to Rowdil in the Isle of Harris, properties were endowed upon the Canons. At Rowdil the Lord of Isles built them that remarkable church that has long outlived the mother foundation. The Isles of Colonsay and Oransay were theirs. Fergus, the fierce and formidable Lord of Galloway, was one of their earliest benefactors : after years spent stubbornly maintaining the independence of his Province against the Scottish king, Fergus rode to Edinburgh, to sanctuary in Holyrood, where he became a monk. After him many other warriors, grown weary, faced the last, inner struggle as monks of Holyrood. Although, indeed, one of the best of its abbots, Abbot Bellenden, sought his peace by renouncing the Holyrood abbacy to become a " Chartour-monk."

Chronicles were written. Music was composed. It seems certain that the music written in the abbeys was the basis of the traditional tunes of Scotland. From the earliest times the Abbey gardens were cultivated and planted with onions and cabbages, beans and garlic, apples, pears, plums, and strawberries, roses and primroses and gillyflowers : a pleasant contrast with the wild heights to the south and east. Building abbots added to and embellished the precincts.

Forbye, there was the Canongate Burgh and its regality to administer, and bridges to be built across the Water of Leith. There was merchandise : all manner of foreign imports, and wool and hides and fish and grain to send out from Leith. The monks owned the fisheries off the Isle of May. They had mills and breweries—and, indeed, to this day the reek of new beer is associated with Holyrood.

Long before the building of the Palace, the Kings of Scotland were constant visitors. James II, nicknamed "Fiery Face" because of a birthmark, spent most of his thirty years with the Canons, and was born, crowned, married, and buried at Holyrood. A Flemish chronicler describes his wedding feast, with a boar's head served surrounded with tow and bearing thirty-two small flags with the arms of himself and his lords : the tow set alight to the great delight of the company. And a silver ship, fully rigged, was carried in front of the Earl of Orkney, the King's Admiral.

But by now mediæval man was stricken by renaissance pangs. As Voltaire conceded : however bad the Church at any given time, it has always been somewhat better than its circumambience. No doubt the decline in the conduct of the Canons and their Abbots was more than matched by the increasing disorder of the world about them. It was none the less disastrous for that. Things were far from happy when Canons were involved in murderous brawls with the sailors of Leith. The Pope momentarily took matters in hand in 1450, and appointed an Abbot of his own choosing : Archibald Crawford "a priest of the diocese of St. Andrews, Master of Arts, of a race of barons and knights," a promising choice, and one that did not fail. Crawford was about the last of the building Abbots : the flying buttresses that, truncated, still support the walls of the Church are his, and his sculptured arms remain in many places. During the next abbacy, that of the worthy Bellenden, the Holyrood *Ordinale* was written : a fine parchment folio now shown in the Palace gallery. Bellenden was likely the builder of the Chapel of St. Anthony whose ruin stands picturesquely on the Salisbury Crags behind the Abbey. He founded a hospital for the poor and performed other good works of which, it was said, that such was the age that they made him unpopular with "sindry uther prelatis" so that he became a Carthusian monk. His successor, Crichton, a kinsman of the Admirable Crichton, was the last good Abbot, then nepotism brought nemesis. First came one of the Douglases, brother to that Earl of Angus who had married Margaret Tudor, widow of James IV, and had the boy king in his keeping. Then came Robert Cairncross, a shocking upstart schemer who gained the post by the old ruse of betting with the young James that he would not get the next preferment. Now disorder emanated from the

Abbey instead of order. The Canons actually themselves raided and razed the chapel of the Blackfriars in Edinburgh. Two reformers were tried in the Abbey and burnt. The Provost of Edinburgh had to protest against the levying of a penny on every full cart coming up the Canongate into his burgh. The conduct of the Abbot and his Canons became generally scandalous, and nothing was left but for James to nominate his infant bastard to the once honourable post of Abbot of Holyrood.

III

The symmetry of the main front of the Palace of Holyroodhouse (18) can give, at first sight, a quite wrong notion of its building. The present effect is the work of Sir William Bruce, who was a master at adapting earlier fabrics into a homogeneous concept of his own. The entry is flanked by two tower blocks, each capped with twin turrets. But whereas the northern one (19) is the James IV Tower of 1500, its opposite number is Bruce's work of the reign of Charles II. In the century and a half that elapsed between the building of the original tower and the building of its twin, the Palace went through various changes. In fact, although James IV was pushing his ingenious Master Mason, Leonard Logy, a cleric and probably a Canon of the Abbey, to have enough finished to make a good show for his bride, whom he married in 1503, the topmost part of the Tower was still incomplete when he was killed at Flodden ten years later. The original plan was the familiar L plan of the more developed Scottish tower—often called a Place or Palace even when having no association with royalty. The King's cousin, the Duke of Albany, came from France to act as Governor of Scotland during the minority of James V, and by 1515 was continuing the work at Holyroodhouse, and later James V made additions under the supervision of Hamilton of Finnart—a typically able and unscrupulous Renaissance character, executed for treason in 1540.

There are records of dainty decoration within the rooms at that time : of coloured walls, with gold or azure borders, and of a symbolic picture by a native painter, John Ross, depicting the Pope, a knight, and a labouring man : of dressed stones shipped across the Forth from Culross, and of rubble from nearer quarries. But most of this work was swept away in the " Rough Wooing "— Hertford's destructive expeditions to forward the efforts of Henry VIII to secure the hand of the infant Mary Stewart for the infant Edward Tudor. Only the weel-biggit Tower of James IV survived.

After Hertford, building went on again. This time the nearest quarry of all was chosen : the Abbey buildings themselves, for the Commendator was in charge, and no respecter of person or property. His own house was a quaint conception, with double-decked dormers, pulled down in 1833. It was nothing like as splendid a bield as the palace which his son, Earl Patrick Stewart, who continued his father's swashbuckling in the Orkneys, built at Kirkwall, and whose ruins retain amazing splendour to this day.

This time the building was in preparation for the return to Scotland of Mary, Queen of Scots and the widow of a few months of the Dauphin. She was nineteen years old, six foot tall, stately, and renowned the loveliest and most accomplished Princess of her time. Peaceful and generous of nature, she came to such a byke of bullies, cowards, and downright double-dyed rogues, as rarely disgraced any kingdom at any time.

Although the Palace had been enlarged, it was still inadequate for the accommodation of a complete Court. Mary had to take over a house from Lord Ruthven in the Abbey Close for the over-flow. Yet it must have been impressive enough, for it received praise from tourists from abroad, who were no doubt connoisseurs of what was befitting a royal residence. Later, James VI before his return visit in 1617, commanded with proper conceit that Holyrood should be redded up " in respect he would be convoyit and conducted be certain noblis of Ingland he wald let them know that this cuntrie was nothing inferior to theirs in anie respect." James further wanted the chapel to be enriched by Inigo Jones, with gilded wood carvings of the twelve apostles and a pair of organs : but the Scottish bishops, for fear of the Presbyterian element in Edinburgh, dissuaded him.

From its beginnings, when James IV first started migrating his Court from Linlithgow and the exquisite little palace his father had built in the old Royal Castle of Stirling, the Palace of Holyroodhouse had been a Stewart home. The Stewarts always maintained their interest in it and affection for it. Charles I had begun making alterations when he started upon his ill-advised ecclesiastical alterations, which put an end to his intentions at Holyrood, and eventually to his own life. It was left to Charles II to complete the building as we know it to-day.

His consideration for Holyrood is the more remarkable as he never actually set foot in it. Yet he took personal interest in the work which he entrusted to one of the greatest of Scotland's architects, Sir William Bruce of Balcaskie, the contemporary of Sir Christopher Wren. Under Bruce was Robert Milne, of that

16 Darnley's Audience Chamber

17 A William Bruce interior

HOLYROODHOUSE INTERIORS

18   The Palace of Holyroodhouse

19   The James IV Tower, from the foot of the Canongate

long line of King's Master Masons. The King inspected all the plans and made many modifications. He imperatively ordered the removal of a central doorway and entablature that had been added by the command of Oliver Cromwell as part of necessary renovations after Monck's troops, who were stationed there, had, in the traditional manner, accidentally set fire to their barracks. He wrote to Bruce : " With all possible diligence you shall demolish and take down the buildings and rooms built by the usurpers above the front of the west quarter and designe and order the building thereof in pillar work conforme to and with the Dorick and Ionic orders and finishe the ends above the platform of the front order, agreeing with the Corinthian style."

Renaissance classical was not intolerant of the old Tower, only demanding the enlarging of its windows, which necessitated alterations in the floor levels and some changes in the intramural stairs. Beyond that, its repetition at the south end of the front was deemed sufficient for its formalising. The long leg of the L, however, with its crenellations and its high diamond-paned windows, was entirely changed, given a more austere façade and made to serve as a screen to bind the flanking towers (19). In the centre the main entrance leads into the courtyard, through Doric pillars and beneath the Royal Arms. The whole front is 215 feet long, and the inner quadrangle 94 feet square. Bruce had some scheme for the quadrangle which Charles considered " very noble," but too expensive, and eventually it was carried out in the present modest but effective courses of Doric, Ionic, and Corinthian pilasters, for the first, second, and third floors respectively. The rear of the eastern range, facing over the lawns and gardens that replaced the Abbey ruins, was carried out to the same design. The marble chimney pieces were sent up from London, and a Dutch painter of modest talent, Jacobus de Wet, was employed to paint portraits of real and imaginary kings of Scotland by the yard. These portraits still decorate the Gallery. Now and again there are heated denunciations of them, and suggestions that they should be displaced and the Gallery more elegantly decorated. True, they darken a fine room : but they have earned some right of tenancy, and if they lack beauty they have humour—there is a nice touch of the ridiculous about King Fethelmacus and his kin.

From 1679 until 1682 James was resident in Holyrood as Commissioner, the last time royalty has been resident in Scotland in any official capacity. Religious *sturm und drang* dominates the period in the history books : but it is on record that it was one long looked back upon in Edinburgh as an oasis of vitality and

promise, and indeed it would be difficult to overrate the importance to a Capital city of a royal focus in those times. James took
a keen interest in the amenities of his Palace, and amongst other
things held theatrical entertainments in the tennis court, to the
scandalising of the puritannical element.

IV

James IV was certainly a remarkable personality, but it is an
erroneous picture that sometimes credits him with stimulating
a sudden brief-lived golden age for Scotland, and particularly in
the world of literature. Indeed, Hector Boece laments his lack
of letters and learning, which the historian recalls were much
better served under the poet king, James I. But the poets of
the period 1500 were more fortunate than their predecessors,
and much more of their work remains to us, giving it a false
impression of isolation.

James IV suffered from a familiar Scottish complaint, the love
of novelty. At Holyrood he paid far more attention to the needs
and luxuries of John Damien, an international adventurer who
arrived in Edinburgh with all the tricks of his trade, than to
those of the outstanding poet about the Court, William Dunbar.
Damien introduced him to such playocks as the delights of
experimental surgery. " A false card up Damien's sleeve " was
of more account to the King than poetry, complained Dunbar.
There was, of course, method in his complaint ; and that it
eventually was successful does credit to James.

Dunbar's poems of the Court give vignettes of life at Holyrood
at the time. It is a life of hearty rather than elegant enjoyment.
At the dancing in the Queen's chaumer the high spot seems to be
the clamant breaking of wind that the exercise of the dance
induces. The King was active as ruler, administrator, amorist,
diplomat on the European stage, penitent and pilgrim. As a
general he failed, and he and the flower of Scotland were killed at
Flodden. Once more the Stewart fate was manifest : but this
time it was truly fatal for Scotland. If he, or indeed either of his
equally able and gifted predecessors, James I or James II, had
lived to be sixty, our history must almost certainly have been
totally changed. As it was, the unifying effect of the monarchy
was lost under recurrent royal minorities, and at the last those
noblemen of extraordinary rapacity and duplicity brought the
kingdom to ruin. Like unleashed gauleiters or commissars,

plotting and intriguing, murdering and robbing, they set a pace for crime that was to prepare the way for a creed of despair, and with it to stultify Scottish life for centuries.

Degenerate although the Church was, it was patriotic, vastly more principled than the noble laity even while James V was hastening its decline. His mother, Margaret Tudor, had much in common, including a taste for marriage, with her brother, Henry VIII, who was so near bringing his own kingdom to ruin. As Queen she was succeeded very briefly by the daughter of the French king, who died in Holyrood, and then by the second wife of James V, the noble Mary of Lorraine, who, when a widow, tried herself to hold the fast-slipping power of the throne until her daughter's return from sanctuary in France.

With Mary Stewart we come to those scenes in Holyrood that above any other give the Palace its renown far furth of Scotland. I remember a day in July, 1945, meeting in Holyrood with a company of players, the Comédie Française on their memorable visit to Edinburgh. To them almost the only interest the Palace held was in its association with Mary Queen of Scots. The figure of a lovely woman, a queen, set in a swirl of murder and puritan-nical outcry, has an immediate ring of romance. But, whereas Romance may often attach itself with uncalled-for flourish to events not in themselves of great significance, in the case of Mary of Scots and of John Knox, the romance dwindles before the magnitude of reality. Even were it not irresistible I believe I should be justified in devoting some pages to a story which more than any other illustrates our history, ethos, and perhaps what Hugh MacDiarmid has called the Caledonian antisysygy : the conflict that has exacerbated our character and defines the living history of the country of which Edinburgh is Capital.

V

Nothing requires so much justifying as a crime. But few crimes can have had so vast a legacy of justification as those of which Mary Stewart was victim. And the reason that has made even worthy persons calumniate her memory for 350 years is a mistaken zeal for the defence of John Knox. It is assumed that if Knox is discredited the whole Kirk of Scotland stands impeached. It is a curious assumption because he did not originate the reformed church, and the Kirk has long dissociated itself from Knox's creed and practice. True, the Westminster Confessional embodies the appalling rigmarole of predestination : but only the small extreme sects, totally separated from the main body of the Kirk, subscribe to the belief, and they themselves would never adopt Knox's liturgy or regular communion.

In fact, it would be difficult for anyone to make a case that Knox did other than pervert the Scottish Reformation. But for him there is no reason why it should not have come in comparatively peacefully, as in other countries, preserving much that was good, and bringing even some such renaissance as it did in England. In Scotland the impossible creed of Knox created an intellectual vacuum from which his Church can scarcely be said to have recovered. Dr. Johnson could justly trounce the Presbyterians for their lack of theology : political diatribe remained for long the essence of almost everything they wrote. Knox only returned to Scotland after the Reformation was established. He was its saboteur rather than its genius.

The receding waves of the years have revealed the jetsam of Knox's perjury. He went further than his master, Calvin, in deliberately inciting the mob to the destruction of churches and their furnishings. Later, in his dishonest "History of the Reformation," because such destruction had proved unpopular, he disclaimed responsibility. But his letters remain to damn him. He was a spy for the English and their hired tool. It is argued that in this he was using what means he could to forward the ends in which he believed. The argument is thin : and it leaves him a quisling, that is, a self-justified traitor. He was a demagogue and a liar : a man of violence who did not mind flatly contradicting himself when it suited him. For this in his defence it is always argued that one must consider the times in which he lived. But while that argument has a certain weight applied to the smaller fry of any period, it is simply unacceptable in the case of any man who presumes to be a Christian leader. The manners and the style and the accent of the Christian leader will vary in different times and places, but Christianity itself remains as constant as its Founder. John Knox was courageous only in the way of a fanatic. He set up as the champion of morals, but spared the guilt of those who were useful to him while he scourged the innocence of his opponents. Never in his active life does Knox reveal a vestige of charity. When he stood before Mary in the Palace of Holyrood he, who claimed to follow the prisoner before Pilate, was simply a hectoring, offensive bully. He set up to be a prophet, and no doubt excused his cant by a sense of trance in the loom of his verbosity. But what shall it avail a man if he prophesy and have not charity ?

20   The Old Town from Princes Street

From the print by A. Kay (1812)

His most successful prophecy was to foretell a murder to which he was privy. His most important prophecies were refuted. In fact the Reformation that was his cause, as it was the cause of the Covenanters who followed him, was a failure. For the Scottish Reformation was not like the English. In England the Reformers were content to consider that they had cleaned up that part of the Universal Church that was on English soil. They might burn and express contempt for the papists : they did not assume the responsibility of reforming the world. But the Scots were not so temperate. It was essential to Knox's creed that it should spread : that Edinburgh was the new Jerusalem with a vengeance, from whence newly discovered truth was to spread across the whole world. History emphatically refuted his revelation, and Scotland paid an appalling price for his presumption.

Knox in this shows himself the complete idealogue, comparable to the doctrinaire Marxian of to-day, his enthusiasm for theory flexing his principles to any treachery. A theory by which it was necessary that none before should ever have been so good or so wise as his enlightened. Of Wishart he said in his later days, " a man of such graces as before him were never heard within this realm, yea, and are rare to be found yet in any man, notwithstanding this great light of God that since his days has shined unto us." Already, one suspects, a shudder of doubt, or at least of ire that for all his ministry no bright light of Godliness shone amongst the ministry and layfolk of Edinburgh. But he would not have recognised it if it had been there, for, confronted by Mary, he had cried her Jezebel.

The kindest possible attitude to John Knox is to accept in him a symptom of sickness and national degradation. His creed of predestination reflects the fatalism and despair of Scotland in his time. It was a despair that afflicted him so much that only his overweening vanity gave him the strength to push his reforms to their bitter end. It is pertinent that such doctrinaire Calvinism as is left in Scotland is confined to the extreme secessions which came out of the larger establishments after the oppressive horrors that culminated in the Highland Clearances, amongst those to whom again there appeared to be no hope against a malignant fate : no redress, no justice, no goodwill. It is the last ditch of resistance against the apathy of complete defeatism.

John Knox, old and almost pathetic, cried in dreadful accents of doubt and vainglory in one of his last sermons in St. Giles : " What have I been to my country, albeit this unthankful age will not know, yet the ages to come will be compelled to bear witness to the truth ! "

23

David Hume bore witness that fanatical puritanism in Scotland was Knox's endowment. Writing of his letter to the Catholics from Perth, Hume says : " With these outrageous symptoms commenced in Scotland that hypocrisy and fanaticism which long infected that kingdom, and which, though now mollified by the lenity of the civil power, is still ready to break out on all occasions." John Wesley in his *Journal* makes a second pertinent judgment, in expressing surprise that the Scottish Kirk was not more vitiated than it was by its exegesis. " *Monday 23rd June,* 1766. We rode in a mild, cool day to Thorny-Hill, about sixty measured miles from Glasgow. Here I met with Mr. Knox's History of the Church of Scotland : and could any man wonder if the members of it were more fierce, so sour, and bitter of spirit than some of them are ? For what a pattern have they before them ! I know it is commonly said, " The work to be done needeth such a spirit." Not so : the work of God does not, cannot need the work of the Devil to forward it."

VI

JOHNSON : " Sir, never talk of your independency, who could let your queen remain twenty years in captivity and then be put to death without even a pretence of justice, without your ever attempting to rescue her ; and such a Queen, too !—as every man of any gallantry of spirit would have sacrificed his life for."

WORTHY MR. JAMES KER (Keeper of the Records) : " Half our nation was bribed by English money."

JOHNSON : " Sir, that is no defence : that makes you worse."

From the stage where it was deemed necessary to justify Knox's calumny and make Mary out as a monster of lechery and murder, we have passed to an age in which Knox's purpose is largely forgotten, and many of the charges against Mary have been relinquished. They were always false charges, first made by those who were paid to make them or who, guilty themselves, had excellent reason as well as political motive for accusing her. In fact there was never any evidence to connect her with the murder of Darnley, and plenty of evidence of her innocence.

The charge against Mary that dies hardest, however, concerns her relationship with Bothwell. The fantastic stories of her letch for him before Darnley's death have been disproved. The Casket Letters have been shown to have been forgeries—as far as is humanly possible, seeing that nobody except the plotters themselves was ever allowed to see the originals : so that virtually

24

they never existed except by the testimony of a lot of interested rogues, who dare not even show them to Queen Elizabeth because she knew her cousin's handwriting. The simple facts of History reveal the marriage with Bothwell as a case of abduction, common enough in those days and for long after, in which marriage was the only course left to the victim unless she had friends at hand to save her : and Mary had none. In fact, Mary had reason to put her trust in Bothwell, howsoever reluctantly, for he had been more loyal to her and to Scotland than any of his fellow nobles.

To-day, however, it is rather the fashion to condone and to explain than to accept the evidence refuting the charges of lust. Even writers of repute weave theories of current jargon around her, and consider that they write in her defence. Eric Linklater finds the evidence of her lust so manifestly disproved that he considers that she must have been " under-sexed." Margaret Irwin makes a novelettish romance out of Bothwell's abduction : all justified by " lerve." It is certainly true that nothing is so difficult for people to accept as straightforward and undissembling conduct. If " under-sexed " means anything, it means presumably some nervous diffidence such as there is no reason to assume that Mary, with her gay disposition and French upbringing, should suffer from. It is almost as though Mr. Linklater should regard continence as an inevitably negative occupation. While Miss Irwin evinces a big-hearted broadmindedness, no doubt, but not her usual discrimination.

Mary describes in her letters to France exactly what befell when Bothwell abducted her. Apart from marriage she could find no " outgait." Her letters have every ring of truth. And there is no evidence that she ever told a lie. Her whole conduct, her tolerance and patience, her lack of any bigotry, endow her with self-evident veracity. Simply to accept the facts of history is to vindicate Mary, not partially but completely. The facts have been admirably collated by that distinguished jurist Sir Edward Parry in his book *The Persecution of Mary Stewart*.

It was in a room of Holyrood that Knox faced Mary. The nineteen-year-old Queen spoke to him with courtesy, lenience, and (on his own testimony) deep understanding. He replied without deference to her position, her sex, or her age : protecting himself from sympathy or understanding or charity by that kind of rant that is the refuge of the cruel or the weak. His words were not apposite nor reasoned but canting, their piety was as false as piety always is when it is used as a political plank. Lack of good manners may not be one of the mortal sins, it is frequently their fruit. It is always easiest for a man to do injustice when he shouts

25

down his own intelligence with insults on his opponents. The picture is of universal significance, like all great tragedy, but it has peculiar pertinence to Scotland. In Mary we have what " every man of any gallantry of spirit " must love : happiness and integrity, dignity and mildness, grace and generosity. In Knox we have that *alter ego* that the Scot so often seems to think he should sustain, because it is dark, seems strong, outspoken, and trumpets morality. And yet he is immoral, because he is a liar : he is false, a traitor ; vain, deeming himself one of the elect ; he is savage, without mercy. He is a figure of gloom and hate masquerading as righteousness, defaming his God.

In trying to swallow Knox, the Kirk has poisoned itself. It will not find the antidote to that venom until it has renounced him, and made recompense to the memory of Mary, whose leniency towards it, and lack of biogtry, lost her the support of the Catholic faction in her own day. She asked only the freedom of conscience to worship as she wished, the Kirk's own claim. Knox died in his bed in the odour of sanctimoniousness. Mary joined that great company of her noblest countrymen on the *via crucis* of ignominious death.

In Mary's room a brass plate marks the spot where Rizzio was murdered. To be precise, it marks a spot some three feet beneath the actual place, since the floor-level was lowered in Charles's alterations. Mary sat at supper when Darnley entered by the private stair, drunk, sat beside her and kissed her. The old dying venomous Lord Ruthven, in full armour, dragged his failing body after Darnley, and stood, with drawn sword and sickly, evil countenance, at the arras by the stair-head. " Judas ! ' Mary whispered to her husband, who replied miserably, " *Ce n'est rien ! Ce n'est rien !* " Mary, heavy with child, rose to protect her friend. Faldonside held his pistol at her breast. She told him to fire if he did not respect her child. Bellenden made a thrust at her with his rapier, which was struck down by a page. Rizzio was stabbed clinging to her dress, then dragged by a noose over his neck into the Presence Chamber, where with barbaric bellowing the murderers slashed and hacked his body to bits. His crime : he was " a merry fellow and a good musician." It is almost certain that Knox was privy to the murder : he has left his own testament that he approved of it. To the credit of the people of Edinburgh they came that night in force to protect their Queen from a plot that may well have been directed also against her own life, and almost certainly against that of her child. The crowd called for her from the Abbey Close, but Ruthven forbad her appear, crying, "Sit down ! If you stir you shall be

21 View from the top of Princes Street in 1824

After the print by J. Gendall

cut in collops and flung over the walls ! ''   And Darnley reassured the mob with lies.

Mary escaped from the Palace the next night, and was little more in Holyrood.   Gone were its days of masques and dances, of the wedding celebrations of the Queen's Maries.   (They married to avoid scandal, the unspeakable Knox thundered from his pulpit in purest tones of premeditated falsehood.)   The rather shabby son who followed her eventually, did himself enjoy entertainments, but his stay in Holyrood was vexed with the extraordinary wrangles thrust upon him by Knox's rabble ministry and by the murderous threats of his half-mad cousin, Bothwell's nephew.   And then James went to London and left Holyrood kingless.

VII

When Prince Charles Edward Stewart came to the Palace in 1745 there were many whose rejoicing was less of loyalty or politics than the sheer happiness of seeing it regally held.   It was a glorious interlude, both for the crowds at the yetts and for the grand folk who danced at the balls.   The following year the Butcher Cumberland made an abrupt, contemptuous stay.

Various noble families, besides the Hereditary Keepers, the Dukes of Hamilton, had rooms in the Palace during its desuetude, and a rather unexpected Royalty joined them in 1796.   This was the Comte d'Artois, subsequently Charles X of France.   Sir Walter Scott was there to mark his royal entry, and to remark upon it with appropriate reference to the Auld Alliance.   His was a curious exile, a double one, for he was avoiding not only the Jacobins but also his creditors.   No place could have been more suitable for such a case than Holyrood, for besides its regal setting it retained one of the rights of sanctuary it had held probably since the days of the Canons.   Monsieur could live in becoming dignity and at the same time avoid the duns.   Of course he could only leave the palace precincts on a Sunday, which he did to go to Mass in the upper chamber that long served as chapel in the Blackfriars' Wynd.   He had to be back within the precincts by midnight.   Those of the Abbey Lairds, as the debtor population of the precincts were familiarly called, who were rash enough to enjoy themselves too late on a Sunday evening were sometimes nabbed by the duns skulking in the shades of the Canongate.   A number of celebrated persons lodged in the boarding houses that were established around the Abbey to accommodate the Lairds.

At one time Edinburgh's Lord Provost was one and De Quincey was another. De Quincey got into the awkward predicament of falling into debt with his Holyrood landlady, and so, being threatened with imprisonment in the Abbey's private gaol, he had to seek sanctuary from sanctuary itself.

For debtors the right of sanctuary survived until the Act of 1880 made it unnecessary. It applied to all the Abbey grounds, where there were many houses until, with Queen Victoria making Holyrood an occasional residence, most were demolished between 1850 and 1860. George IV, incidentally, never stayed at Holyrood, although he entertained there, in a kilt and silk tights. Only Croft-an-Righ and the houses in the Abbey Strand remain. The quaint building known as Queen Mary's Bath was actually one of the turrets along the Abbey wall, whose handsome Foir Yett was unfortunately and for no known reason demolished in 1755 : the raggles of its arcading are still visible on the south side of the Strand.

22   Holyrood, looking towards the Calton Hill

A View of the NETHERBOW PORT of EDINBURGH from the West
This ancient Fabric was taken down 31st of August 176.

23   The demolition of the Netherbow Port in 1764
From a contemporary drawing by A. Runciman

The Mediæval City

The Golden Age—The Walled City—The Puritan Sway—
Queen Mary's Edinburgh

I

EDINBURGH IS VERY MUCH A ROYAL CITY. IT SPRANG UP along, and for long was confined to the ridge running from the Royal Castle and Palace on the rock to the kingly foundation of the Abbey, later with its Palace, at the foot of the slope. It was not really a strategic nor a centred foundation. As a place of intensified habitation it is not old, although there are traces of prehistoric terraced cultivation along the south-eastern slopes of Arthur's Seat and some within the compass of the Old Town itself. Roman civilisation bypassed it altogether. The pleasant Midlothian village of Inveresk was the nearest Roman settlement of importance : a place at once more easily defended than Edinburgh and more genial. The site of Edinburgh would definitely have been an awkward one for colonisers : exposed, at a distance from its river mouth, and with its southern approaches difficult to defend. Duddingston, now within the City bounds, and Dunsappie Hill show evidence of more intensive early habitation, and appear also to have been occupied by the Romans at a later period than Inveresk.

During the ascendancy of Northumbria, all Lothian, comprising Berwickshire as well as East, Mid, and West Lothian, came for a time under the Saxon dominance of Edwin, which has given rise to a theory that the burgh took its name from that Prince. It is, however, far more likely that it is an example of the Gaelic prefix, fairly common in Scotland (cf. Edinample, Edinbane), and signifying a *slope* : the burgh on the slope : certainly entirely appropriate. The Saxon domination of Lothian, the only important Saxon inroad north of the Border, was not of long durance, and was terminated by the bloody victory gained by the Pictish King Brude at Dunnechtan in 685. There was a Christian settlement and a wooden church, perhaps on the site of the present High Kirk of St. Giles, at this time. But little enough is known of the beginnings of Edinburgh until the reign of Malcolm Canmore four hundred years later.

E   29

As has been observed, through his Queen, St. Margaret, Malcolm brought to Scotland the advantages of Norman culture without the disadvantages of Norman conquest, and, despite the customary disputes of succession and provincial independence, he inaugurated a golden age that lasted and waxed for more than two hundred years. It was the period that saw the building of the Abbey and Palace at Dunfermline, of the Abbey at Holyrood, of churches and cathedrals in many parts of the country. It saw a blossoming of civilised life in all its spheres, and generally a substantially more settled era than that prevailing in the sister kingdom of England at the same period. Unfortunately, Edward I, whose evil genius brought an end to our golden age, destroyed even most of the documents that recorded it in detail. It is on the surviving buildings, and on the plans and laws of the old burghs, that we have to rely to gain most of our knowledge of the twelfth and thirteenth centuries in Scotland. The rapid development of the burghs speaks for a widespread increase in trade and prosperity. " The Laws of the Four Burghs " happily remains, one of the oldest civic documents in existence, to give us details of their administration.

As Sir Frank Mears has shown, " the burghs represent only one unit of a threefold one of castle, burgh, and abbey, and this trinity will be found, no doubt with its parts in varying relative scale, to have been adopted in probably every case." In Edinburgh the trinity is most emphatically defined. Sir Frank Mears demonstrates further that the burghs originally were not products of haphazard development but carefully laid out around a central open space which was only encroached upon in later times.

A nucleus of Edinburgh sprang up after the enclosing of the whole summit of the Castle rock. This civilian suburb would extend originally a bow-shot from the gate, spreading down the steep, narrow street of Castle Hill and fanning out at the head of the West Bow, which, with its sharp descent and zig-zag line, developed in the twelfth century and only altered in the last, must have been exceptionally picturesque.

The West Bow led to the Grassmarket, somewhat isolated in its hollow to the south of the Castle (anciently called the King's High Street under the Castle Wall) : but the regular set out of the ancient burgh was based upon a single wide street running east, the houses standing well back from the parish church. Between the houses ran closes (blind alleys) and wynds (open alleys), down to two back lanes, of which that to the south, the Cowgate, the cattle road, remains to this day. Originally there was none of the congestion of later days. The burgh, although a centre of trades and crafts, was much concerned with agricultural and horticultural amenity. Each burgher was a smallholder working a croft of not less than a rood, keeping cattle, pigs, sheep, and poultry, concerning whose proper control new by-laws were constantly introduced. Gordon of Rothiemay's map (29) shows, as late as 1647, the disposition of the Canongate, at that time still a separate burgh, a suburb of Edinburgh, as very much a garden city, with large and finely laid-out pleasances behind the houses of the nobility.

Although none of the domestic buildings of the golden age of Scotland and Edinburgh remain, they were presumably like their counterpart in England and on the Continent; wood-framed, with plaster or clay infilling. Their gables were often turned to the street and their grounds were entered by a gateway to the side. The closes and wynds of to-day perpetuate these original entries. Gate-posts and beams were carved and painted : the infilling was white or colour-washed. Indeed, many of the stone-built churches and castles of that and of far later times were slapped over with harling, a lime and grit rough-cast that emphasised the mouldings of jambs and lintels and corbelled projections. St. Giles kirk seems definitely to have been finished with whitewash.

Edinburgh must have been a gay and delightful sight amongst its gardens : little coloured houses standing back from a grander church, and linking by their length the formidable stronghold of the Castle, high on its rock, and the fine church and conventual buildings of the Canons in the sheltered hollow at Holyrood : a bright and coloured scene in contrast to the stone and smoke-grey Edinburgh of later times.

II

> When Alexander our King was deid
> That Scotland led in law and le,
> Away was sones of ale and breid,
> Of wyne and wax, of gamyn and gle.
> Our golde was changit into leid.
> Christ, born into virginitie,
> Succour Scotland and remeid,
> That stad is in perplexitie.

So the earliest extant piece of Scottish poetry laments the accident that killed Alexander III in the year 1286. It is a heart-cry from a dark age from which in some measure the nation never recovered. Thereafter came the usurpation of the throne by Edward I, and the most bloody and vindictive laying waste of the country. Edinburgh was burnt to the ground. Travellers to Scotland describe a state of forlorn poverty that is too often allowed to obscure the fact that this was the direct product of wars at least as ruinous in their day as are our wars of to-day. There was no incentive to settled communities, scant point in the building of houses or churches when these were liable to immediate destruction. By 1350 the pound Scots had depreciated to one-twelfth of its sterling value. Hitherto it had the same value as the English pound. But from now on it remained in the region of one shilling and eightpence of English money at which it was finally fixed at the Union of the Crowns. That factor is a fair measure of the drastic and persisting effects upon Scotland of the English Wars. The heroic campaigns of Wallace and the Bruce were successful in preserving the identity of Scotland, but it was a costly success and the old prosperity and certitude were not to be recaptured.

Although during the fourteenth century it became a tradition with the English kings to descend upon Edinburgh, demolish all the houses and despoil Holyrood, some part of the Norman church of St. Giles survived all this destruction : in fact the splendidly figured Norman entry was only removed at the end of the eighteenth century. By the latter part of the fourteenth century St. Giles (24, 25) was being reconstructed and enlarged : further additions were made a hundred years later, when James III erected it into a Collegiate church, with a provost, curate, and sixteen prebendaries. William Preston of Gourton brought from France a relic of the Saint, an armbone, which was treasured until the Reformation, when its reliquary was sold. But Preston's arms remain, in acknowledgment of his gift, on the roof of the choir.

It should be remarked that in Catholic days, St. Giles was never a Cathedral, being under the Archbishopric of St. Andrews which had its own magnificent cathedral church. It only became a Cathedral for a very brief period under Episcopacy, until taken over by the Presbyterians who at that time did not admit the existence of cathedrals.

Great vitality and fervour is shown by the constant rehabilitation of the burgh church in the face of such repeated destruction. Little else was left of the town during those times. When first Edinburgh seems to emerge again in some shape it is with the building of the King's Wall by James II in 1450. It is now a walled city, on the defensive (27). It is noteworthy that the wall actually enclosed a smaller area than the burgh had occupied during the golden age. For it is pretty clear that the closes even

24 The interior

25 The nave looking west

ST GILES'S

26 Edinburgh from the Dean. *After an engraving by Slezer*

27 A map of Edinburgh done in the early seventeenth century

to the south of the Cowgate are part of the original foundation, while the King's Wall was well above the Cowgate, running close to the present front of the Parliament House. It was a considerable reduction of the total area, but gave strategic height to the defences. However, expansion thereafter must have been rapid, for in the panic that followed the disastrous defeat and death of James IV at Flodden, a new wall was rapidly built to protect an area lying well south of the Cowgate. In fact the Cowgate had become a popular suburb, and it long retained the decayed remnants of once splendid houses.

The Flodden Wall is important in the history of Edinburgh, for long defining the City bounds. Nor, for some 250 years, did the people risk building themselves houses outside it, but instead, as the population increased, piled storey upon storey to a height that made Edinburgh unique amongst the cities of Europe : the skyscraper community of its day. They reached eventually nine or ten storeys, and some of the " lands " may have had up to fourteen from the lower level of the back-lanes from which their walls towered up to 130 feet in height. It should be added that some archivists dispute those figures with considerable warmth : but they certainly have some contemporary support.

The Flodden Wall ran south from the south-east corner of the Castle rock across the end of the Grassmarket to which it struck a parallel line below Heriot's Hospital, bulging out to enclose the Greyfriars' Church, ran above the head of Candlemaker Row, by the Kirk o' Field (the site of the University), and turned north again just short of the Pleasance. It followed the march between Edinburgh and Canongate and turned west near the site of the Waverley Station to where its place was taken by the waters of the Nor' Loch which served to protect the City from the north. It was an elaborate structure of considerable height, with towers, crenellations, loop-holes, and embrasures. Its gateways were heavily defended. They were the West Port at the end of the Grassmarket : the Bristo Port : the Cowgate Port : and the Netherbow Port (23) at the Canongate. Below the Netherbow Port the wall was formed of the houses on the west side of Leith Wynd, whose inhabitants, in time of danger, were bound to block doors and windows opening on the wynd. There was a slight extension of the wall north in 1560, to enclose Trinity College, whose lovely little church had been founded by Mary of Gueldres in 1462, and whose site is now a mesh of L.N.E.R. railway lines : and a second small extension south up the Vennel to include the High Riggs, in 1622. A portion of this extension remains alongside Heriot's, which was erected

F   33

shortly afterwards on the burgh's new territory here. Otherwise the Flodden Wall remained unchanged as the boundary of the City until the expansion into the New Town in the eighteenth century.

The earliest reliable map of Edinburgh extant illustrates in semi-elevation an attack from the north, presumably that of the Earl of Hertford in 1544. It (probably inaccurately) shows the Cowgate as almost as wide and important a thoroughfare as the High Street. Dominant buildings are St. Giles, the Kirk o' Field, and the main gateway of the Netherbow Port. Wynds intersect the three blocks of building, and small houses have encroached upon the precincts of St. Giles. The Castle stands aloof, and the Canongate is a somewhat jumbled suburb outside the wide-stretching walls of the Abbey and Palace. It was after this assault that a Palace was again built within the impregnable defences of the Castle. One interesting point suggested by the colouring of this map is that the houses within the City were roofed with red pantiles, while those outside were thatched, possibly slated. Certainly, the Burgh Records contain bye-laws forbidding the theeking of houses within the City, consequent upon fires caused by sparks in the thatch. The slightly later plan (1567), prepared by an English spy reporting the murder of Darnley, gives other clues to architectural detail : a great number of crow-stepped gables and of outside stairways to the houses. The kirk of the Blessed Mary of the Fields is by this time left a roofless ruin.

Hertford, as Duke of Somerset, returned for a second attack three years after his first, but on neither occasion did he succeed in taking the Castle. Edinburgh suffered dreadfully in 1544, in spite of the courageous defence of its citizens. The house-fronts of timber, cut in the Forest of Drumsheugh, blazed furiously after the order to fire the City. But the Laird of Stanehouse drove off all attacks on the Castle, killing some 500 of Hertford's men, and making a successful sortie in which some of the cannon captured were Scottish pieces that had been lost at Flodden. Stanehouse was equally successful in holding the Castle on the second assault, when there was much less of Edinburgh to destroy. He was killed a year or two later in one of the many street fracas that took place in the lacerated and demoralised City.

III

The state of affairs prevailing in some countries of Europe after the second World War is not unlike that of Scotland in the sixteenth century. It would be difficult to exaggerate the demoralisation, the lack of confidence in Church and State, the vitiation of principle that prevailed. It was not merely the widespread destruction, the blitzkrieg tactics of Hertford's armies, and the resultant slaughter and famine: one must remember that the process of attrition had now gone on for centuries. There had been no certain state of peace since the thirteenth century, while the extraordinary series of accidents by which the Kingdom constantly came under the rule of a minor stimulated faction, the regime of gangster noblemen, and weakened again and again the power of a central government.

A Border foray made from Scotland rarely reached any important English centre, and never the Capital itself: but Edinburgh, and about it much of the richest country of Scotland, was easily accessible to an English army.

Taking all things into account, it is at least as remarkable that Scotland should have retained a thrawn core of independence, as that she should have been so rich in traitors and thugs during this momentous century. By 1560 the Reformation was fairly established. The Queen Dowager, Mary of Lorraine, was riding the storm, with some success, until the return of her daughter from France. As yet the Reformation was tolerably orderly and moderate, based upon the Lutheran doctrines of which the *Gude and Godlie Ballates* are a creditable expression. From that alone it can be seen that there was a liberal and cultured quality to the initial Reformation, and one that might reasonably have provided some stimulus to the arts in Scotland similar to that expressed by the English renaissance. But, of course, England's state was entirely different, she had not suffered the oppression that had owrehaillit Scotland. The Calvinism of Knox was a direct expression of the sense of defeat and frustration. Knox was its exponent, but the way was made for him by English bad-neighbourliness. It was no chance that he was in the employment of his country's ancient enemy. Even if he had not been Cecil's tool and spy, he would still have owed his success to England.

In former days when Calvinists (or the upholders of Calvinism, for Scotland has had comparatively few who have accepted the doctrine of Calvin for many generations) supported the Kirk against the criticism that it had impoverished the arts of the nation, so denying it that fine fruit that should have been an earnest of its civilisation, their defence was that the Kirk was concerned with more important matters. They argued that any Church must of its nature be more concerned with the salvation of souls than with the pursuit of the arts. It was a perfectly sound argument, although, of course, with the answer that puritanism

35

can be at least as pernicious to the soul as aesthetic dalliance. To-day, however, the defenders of Knox lack their master's confidence. In fact, after starvation, they have been surfeited by the propagandists of the aesthetic ideal, and they are not nearly so certain about the soul. And so we have such remarkable defences of Knox as that in Mr. Finlay's recent volume on Scotland in the Oxford University Press series. So determined is Mr. Finlay in his defence that he states with more daring than wisdom that Knox and Presbyterianism positively did not harm the arts in Scotland !

No doubt there have been many irresponsible strictures upon Knox and Presbyterianism, made by persons to whom the values that Knox, however unworthily and ineptly, sought, meant nothing. But to suggest that Knox and the ministers did not destroy and frustrate the aesthetic expression of the country is to accuse them of a failure in their own intentions of which, at least, they were not guilty. John Knox himself would not be grateful to his aesthetic defenders. He deliberately encouraged his Reformers in the destruction of church ornament. Much architecture, sculpture, and painting of great beauty was therefore destroyed and lost to the country. Whatever the inherent merits of the earlier Presbyterian kirks, and it is certainly undiscriminating to attack their baldness and overlook their dignity and repose, by their rejection of adornment they did, in a religious age, withdraw most important sanction from aesthetic expression. It is significant that almost the only evidence that Mr. Finlay can adduce in defence of his irrational contention is the silverwork of the seventeenth century communion cups. These are indeed of great beauty, continuing the pre-Reformation tradition with appropriate modification. They offered practically the only scope for the artist-craftsman left by the Reformed Kirk, and therefore aptly serve to prove that the skill and judgment were there, and that it was the Kirk that suppressed its manifestation in other spheres.

Sculpture and painting were both victims of the Kirk's ban. Psalm-singing was permitted, but no music was allowed in the churches until well on in the last century. Architecture suffered least. The Gothic tradition was dying anyway, and much modification is apparent in the last pre-Reformation work, excellent though it is. Later the classical style was austere enough to be acceptable. For secular building the great tradition of Scottish masons remained : there were always noblemen and wealthy merchants who wanted handsome homes for themselves, and they could build them without obvious transgression against puritan-

A general view of the City & Castle of EDINBURGH, the Capital of Scotland.

London, Published by Alex. Hogg at the King's Arms No. 16 Paternoster Row

Morris sculp.

28 A general view of Edinburgh from the south. *After an engraving by Morris*

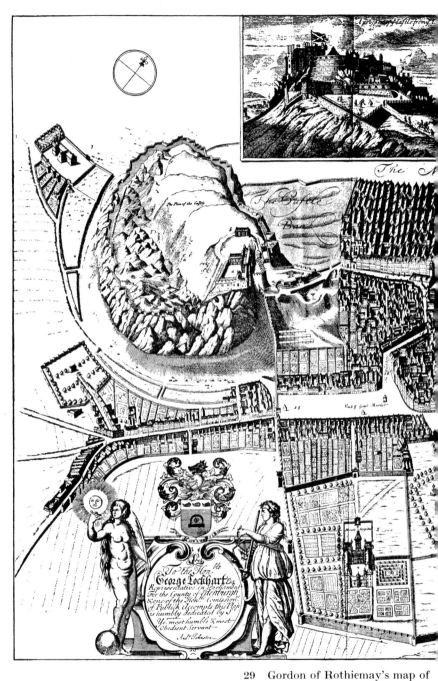

To the Honble

George Lockhart Esq.
Representative in Parliament
For the County of Edinburgh
& One of the Honble Comission-
of Publick Accompts this Plan
is humbly dedicated by Your
Ye most humble & most
Obedient Servant

Ja. Gordon

The Plan of the Castle

The Castle Bank

The Plan of the Castle

29   Gordon of Rothiemay's map of

Edinburgh, 1647.   *As re-engraved after de Wit, 1710*

30 " The Parliament Close and Public Characters Fifty Years Since " (showing St. Giles and the Parliament House before they were re-faced). *An engraving of 1864, from a painting : the figures by Sir David Wilkie, Alexander Fraser and William Kidd, the architecture by David Roberts, John Wilson and others*

ical codes. Literature suffered perhaps first and foremost through the rigorous suppression of the drama by the Kirk. The drama is an obvious stimulus for other arts besides its own. To literature in particular it serves as a vitalising matrix. The history of the Theatre in Edinburgh is one long battle between its exponents and the Kirk from the Reformation even into the last century. For generations the Kirk was consistently victorious. Forbye, the Puritan background was not conducive to the grace or gaiety that are the best inspiration of poetry. Such solitary figures as Drummond of Hawthornden were Episcopalians who strongly disliked the intolerance of the Established Church. Volumes of dull, dreary, uninspired, and singularly untheological tracts and sermons were the chief output of the Scottish presses for a long age.

Thus it is that of the long period that in London saw the first night of *Hamlet* ; the learned satire of Ben Jonson ; the wit of Congreve and Farquhar ; the printing of the poems of Herbert, Donne, Milton, Dryden, Pope, and so many more ; there is almost nothing remotely comparable to be recorded in the life of Edinburgh. It is by no means the whole picture, of course ; for one can make too much even of the best of such expressions of civilisedness ; but it is a sad gap. In the country districts, in the Highlands especially, where the Puritans were long in gaining an ascendancy that they have held the more surely since, poetry was written, or at least composed and recited. The lovely heritage of the Scottish ballads belongs to these years. But of more urbane and cultured poetry there is desperately little. Edinburgh survived, the home of lively, intelligent people, and the scene of much of the variety of a city of the time. Puritanism may have sustained her people in their hardship, which is not to say that it was inevitable, but within its iron corsets she could hardly make her full contribution to the graces of civilisation.

IV

Welcome, O Souveraine ! Welcome, O native Quene !
Welcome to your subjects, great and small !
Welcome, I say, even from the verie splene
To Edinburgh, your syttie principall.

In spite of Knox's campaign, the people of Edinburgh welcomed Mary when she arrived from France. She was received, when her ship berthed at the port of Leith, in the house of Andrew Lamb, a prosperous merchant. The house still stands, by far the oldest in Leith, and has recently been restored. There is a sensible notion to turn it into a maritime museum : an amenity at present curiously lacking to such a sea-going people as the Scots.

The Edinburgh to which Queen Mary came must have been largely a new city, so much of what was old having been destroyed in her rough, unsuccessful wooing. The houses were of stone, but in most extra space was gained by the projecting of wood-fronted galleries on beams over the causeway. The first floor was often reached by a forestair of stone, or perhaps of wood. The original plan and layout of the burgh had been much encroached upon: often through the erection of permanent buildings on sites under the timber galleries originally rented as market booths.

There is a romantic school that pictures Mary a wistful figure coming out of a gay Paris to a gloomy Edinburgh. But for Mary, Paris had been by no means entirely gay, nor was Edinburgh entirely gloomy. She herself never disdained her Scottish nationality, nor her Scottish people for all that she suffered at their hands : forbye, she had ever the greatest loyalty from her personal servants here. She was not a woman of snivelling regrets, but one who accepted life simply, bringing gaiety where it was possible, and taking the burden of suffering without imagined might-have-beens. She brought gaiety to Holyrood, and to the pleasant countryside of Little France where she spent summer days. Like James IV, and others of the line, she enjoyed going incognito into the City in the evenings, dressed as a young man.

Merchants' accounts of the period list a considerable and varied import trade that show a taste and a market for luxuries and refinements. Of more chatty documentation, one of the Edinburgh merchants, Birrel, has left us a diary which contains many slants and humours. Birrel flourished throughout Mary's reign, the regency, and James's Scottish years. He records with a chuckle the descent upon the Palace of the sinister Earl of Bothwell, with King James caught trying to escape with his breeks in his hand. He tells in detail of James's rebuke from the ministers and of his retaliatory threat to remove the Capital from Edinburgh, which set the burgesses in a great pother so that they dealt firmly with the theocratic ministry, and humbly solicited the King's pardon. He delights in such novelties as the arrival of a tumbler who hitched his tight-rope to the Crown Steeple of St. Giles and performed his antics before the crowds around the Mercat Cross. And he tells with relish of the tactlessness of a harsh bailiff who, confiscating the goods of a debtor and exposing them at the place of public execution, rashly hung the portraits of King James and

Queen Anne, which had belonged to the debtor's movable estate, on the gibbet. A gesture that so enraged the King that he ordered the suspending of the bailiff in person from the same gibbet.

Our prejudiced historians always conscientiously record that Mary, brought prisoner from Carberry to Edinburgh, was abused by the mob. Mobs, specially where there are demagogues about, will abuse anyone in distress. But the same historians, with the curiously dogged distortion that has affected them from the time when George Buchanan made lying about Mary a profession, customarily do Edinburgh the injustice of omitting the more significant fact that the traitor lords had to hurry Mary to Loch Leven the next day because the better citizens, merchants, and craftsmen of Edinburgh, were gathering to rescue her. Mary, in fact, left with the people a reputation for grace and goodness (as is shown by the popular street ballad that Cecil's minons tried unsuccessfully to suppress), but when the generation that had known her was dead, her reputation became the prey of propaganda, and not until the eighteenth century did a patient librarian in the Advocates' Library have recourse to State Papers and reveal the extraordinary flimsiness of the case that had been constructed against Mary.

Old Town

I

ALTHOUGH ITS ORIGINAL LAY-OUT WAS TO A FAR EARLIER PLAN, and although most of the existing buildings are of later date, the Old Town seems to bear most strongly the stamp of the seventeenth century : of that brisk phase between the Middle Ages and the elegant rationalism that associates itself with the eighteenth century, and that leads in so interesting a fashion to the assured ebullience of the nineteenth.

An account of the High Street and the Canongate is given by Sir William Brereton, an English Puritan who visited Scotland in 1636. Edinburgh had then about 60,000 inhabitants, all living in the Royal Mile, its sixty closes and wynds, and its immediate neighbourhood. Brereton writes of the High Street : " The best paved street with bowther stones (which are very great ones) that I have seen ; the channels are very conveniently contrived on both sides of the streets, so as there is none in the middle ; but it is the broadest, largest and fairest pavement, and that entire, to go, ride, or drive upon. . . . This street is the glory and beauty of this city : it is the broadest street (except in the Low Countries, where there is a navigable channel in the middle of the street) and the longest street I have seen. . . . The suburbs (Canongate) make an handsome street ; and indeed the street, if the houses, which are very high, and substantially built of stone (some five, some six stories high), were not lined to the outside and faced with boards, it were the most stately and graceful street that ever I saw in my life. . . . This lining with boards and this encroachment into the street about two yards, is a mighty disgrace unto it, for the walls (which were the outside) are stone ; so, as if this outside facing of boards were removed, and the houses built uniform all of the same height, it were the most complete street in Christendom. This city is placed in a dainty healthful pure air, and doubtless were a most healthful place to live in, were not the inhabitants most sluttish, nasty and slothful people . . . only the nobler and better sort of them brave, well-bred

40

31 The Lawnmarket and the spire of Tolbooth St. John's

32 Lintel of 1643 in the Cowgate

33 Lintel in the Canongate

34 Wardrop's Court

35 Gladstone's Land

men, and much reformed." He further observes a vastly equipped public brewhouse, and in Leith many Highlanders in their plaids.

There are still a fair number of the houses that Brereton saw on his visit, and a good many more of an almost identical character. Immediately on the far side of the Esplanade from the Castle, standing at the head of Castle Hill, the first unit of the Royal Mile, stands Cannonball House. In its wall, facing the Castle, reposes a cannonball not very convincingly reputed to have been fired by old General Preston's artillery in the '45. Above is a dormer window with the initials of the builder, one Alexander Mure, a furrier, and his wife, and the date 1630. It has both corbie-stanes and an outside stair. A little farther down and on the opposite side, the Outlook Tower is a structure of the same period, but altered beyond recognition. It now houses an untidy museum and the Camera Obscura, whose ghostly reflected view of Edinburgh was a great delight to my childhood (I always hoped to see some horrible crime enacted on a roof-top, the perpetrator presuming himself safe from all eyes, but forgetting—the Camera Obscura !). The Outlook Tower faces an old five-storeyed block, Boswell's Court, the home of the doctor uncle of James Boswell, which bears a mutilated text of a kind common in the Mile : *O lord in the is al mi trust.*

Lower down, and on the north side again, stood the most interesting of all the Castle Hill buildings, the Palace of Mary of Lorraine, demolished in 1846 to clear a site for the erection of the Free Kirk College that faces down the Mound. It was tenanted by the Queen Regent, near the safety offered by the Castle, immediately after the holocaust of 1544. It was full of carved panelling and richly decorated ceilings, a fitting home, with its view and gardens down the northern slope, for the Queen who preserved such piety and mildness in the grim age in which she lived in Scotland. Some of the woodwork is preserved, and a door with portraits of the Queen and James V is in the Antiquaries Museum.

Castle Hill terminates with Tolbooth St. John's, the Gothic Revival church facing into the Lawnmarket (55), the second constituent element in the Royal Mile. It was originally the " Landmarket," the place where the landward, or country people, had their stalls on market days. It was formerly bounded on the west by the Butter Tron, or weigh-house, and on the east by the tolbooth, that amiably grim gaol : and formed the largest open space in the City, bar the Grassmarket. The merchants were of good standing and maintained a Lawnmarket Club that was the first with intelligence posted from London and beyond. To-day the Lawnmarket is still particularly attractive, with many of its old houses and closes. The most interesting of them all stood at the head of the Upper Bow, entry to the original line of the West Bow (68), an elaborately timbered building whose appearance is still recorded in the colophon of Messrs. Nelson. Like many another, it was pulled down on the grounds that it was unsafe, and then required dynamite to destroy it. It had some fine interiors, and the exterior was the richest remaining example of timber-fronting. Mercifully the nearby Gladstone's Land (35), which is perhaps architecturally the more satisfying, if not so quaint and interesting, was lately preserved through the good offices of an Edinburgh citizen working through the National Trust for Scotland. It has been well restored, and has become appropriately the home of the Saltire Society. The ashlar face of Gladstone's Land rises sheer, and has never squeezed timber galleries out across the pavement. The first floor is arcaded, the last street arcading to be left in Edinburgh, with two bold arches, unequal in size. A forestair climbs to a doorway beneath an ingenious projection of the turnpike stair. The whole building suggests a cheerful acceptance of being squeezed up against its western neighbour :—the small window on the stair, out of line with those of the main upper floors, the break in the second string-course, and the smallness both of the western arch and of the western gablet of the two that complete the whole with a vigorous roof-line. Inside there are the remains of frescoes, and three open-beam ceilings of Memel pine painted with luscious, hot-coloured fruits. This was a common Scottish form of decoration of the time. The painter of Halbert Gledstanes' ceilings was not perhaps highly tutored, but he had a great feeling for his work and carried it out with gusto and innate judgment. The date 1620 occurs on one of the ceilings.

On the same side are three good courts. Milne's Court (39) was built in 1690, one of the first efforts made to obtain an open space in the congestion. The west side and part of the east have been demolished ; but it is still one of the most picturesque and pleasing cuts in the City, with its two pends penetrating from the head of the Mound into the Lawnmarket ; a fine skyline as you look up coming from the Mound, with a pleasantly gnarled passageway underfoot. One set of steps has a balustrade with a big bell-cast to allow for the passing of the skirts of the grand ladies who once lived here. The Court was built by the Robert Milne who carried out the work at Holyrood under Bruce, and who was one of a family who held with great distinction the post of King's Master Mason for seven generations in direct descent.

James's Court and Wardrop's Court (34) are more ordinary, but they make a good stark showing of old wall-face. They enclose Lady Stair's House, surely one of the world's worst examples of " restoration," in which the original building has been entirely refaced by an architect who must have heartily despised the work of his predecessor.

James's Court was erected by a speculative builder in 1725. The western block, which was destroyed by fire, contained the flat that was for long the home of David Hume and that in which Boswell entertained Dr. Johnson. Blocks of flats are an ancient institution in Edinburgh, where they were originally known as " lands." The lands came into being on account of the congestion : it might be said that they supplied land where there was a lack of it. They were notable as often housing the nobility and the artisan under the same roof. There was commonly much good-neighbourliness amongst the tenants : and parties given to those who shared the same stair. Certainly David Hume was fond of his lodging in James's Court, which he had purchased shortly before being sent to Paris as Secretary to the Embassy to the great and warm rejoicing of the Parisian intelligentsia. Despite his success and welcome in France, he wrote : " I am sensible that I am misplaced, and I wish twice or thrice a-day for my easy-chair and my retreat in James's Court. Never think . . . that as long as you are master of your own fireside and your own time, you can be unhappy, or that any other circumstance can add to your enjoyment." On his return he wrote to Adam Smith, at work on *The Wealth of Nations* in Kirkcaldy across the Firth : " I am glad to be in sight of you, and to have a view of Kirkcaldy from my windows." Again, he refers to " my old house in James's Court, which is very cheerful and very elegant, but too small to display my great talent for cookery, the science to which I intend to addict the remaining years of my life." And perhaps that was why he eventually moved across the gulf into the New Town.

These tenements were well equipped for springing an innocent surprise upon strangers once popular amongst the occupants of many of the lands. You took your guest in by the front entrance, led him down flight after flight of stairs until he supposed himself in the bowels of the earth, and then showed him out on ground level again, to a street full of life where he might have anticipated " denizens of the infernal regions." It was a trick that could be played on either side of the ridge—and can still be indulged in places like the Council Chambers : although such novelties have somewhat lost caste in this age of hyper-ingenuity.

Hume's first Edinburgh home was across the way, in Riddle's

Court, behind a fine range of early eighteenth century houses of pre-classical-revival character. Some of these houses are of ashlar, some harled, some roofed with pantiles : they are tall, with gablets and stair towers, lively detail against their impressive proportions. Always at the top windows old women sit, interminably watching the life in the Lawnmarket below. There are bits of earlier building behind the street front : they include what was at one time the Roman Eagle Hall, where Burns was entertained by the Masons, with its plaster ceiling dated 1645-6 : and Bailie MacMoran's house of the late sixteenth century, where James VI and his queen were once feasted in 1598. The wealthy Bailie, its builder, was already dead by that time, having been shot through the head by one of the " gentilmane's bairnes " of the High School when the scholars were on strike over the matter of holidays. They had locked themselves into the school premises in the Blackfriars Gardens, shouting " buttery carles " at the Magistrates and Town Officers who tried to storm their stronghold : and young Sinclair, their leader, put a bullet through the Bailie's ingenious brain. Pressure brought by the Sinclairs and their cousins saved the boy to live to respected age and become a knight and the progenitor of the Earls of Caithness. Birrel took a very poor view of the proceedings.

The six-storeyed block at the north-east corner of the Lawnmarket is in poor repair, and except for a pub and shops on the ground floor, deserted. It is of early eighteenth century type and well merits preservation, especially when we look over the way at the vacuity of the New Sheriff Court that replaced a block of similar houses in recent years. This is an age that may well occupy itself in preserving what it has inherited from the past, both in the way of houses and of liberties, since it is ill-adapted to create anything half as worthy in their place.

In its early days the Lawnmarket housed ambassadors from England and elsewhere. Later, prosperous merchants maintained its standing : they are described as having been " a dram-drinking, news-mongering, facetious set of citizens, who met every morn about 7 o'clock, and after proceeding to the post-office to ascertain the news (when the mail arrived), generally adjourned to a public-house and refreshed themselves with a libation of brandy." Besides their reputable news service, they were fond of inventing and spreading rumours for their own entertainment.

Two notable eighteenth century personalities of the Lawnmarket were Deacon Brodie and Peter Williamson. The former was a Jekyll and Hyde character whose housebreaking and

36 A seventeenth-century gable
in the West Bow

37 Advocate's Close

38 The Pend, leading through Smollet's House into St. John Street

39 The Lawnmarket façade of Milne's Court

40 Old houses in the West Bow

shocking ongoings, masked by civic importance and decorum, have always made a favourite tale for his fellow citizens. He came jauntily to his death on the scaffold hard by at the west end of the Luckenbooths. Peter Williamson set up as printer and news vendor and started the first penny post in the City. As a child in Aberdeen he had been a victim of an infamous traffic by which the City Fathers there cheerfully sold the young of the poorer townsfolk as slaves for the American plantations. Eventually escaping, he returned to Scotland, wrote a remarkable account of his adventures, won an action against his native city, and died in 1799, a useful citizen of Edinburgh.

For myself, I remember the Lawnmarket chiefly for the passage through Milne's Court, for the antique shops, where, as a boy, I prowled occasionally to make a change from the bookshops round the corner, for Gladstone's Land, and for pleasant professional dealings with the firm of map-mounters long established in one of the high old buildings, there regaled with stories of the past, stories of the present Mr. Malloch's grandfather who was brought up farther along the street in a land that still housed grand folk and whose mother kept him at home from school on days when there was an execution at the foot of the Lawnmarket.

II

Two modern roadways now cut off the segment of the Mile that contains the scene of most of Edinburgh's history as Capital of Scotland. The original North Bridge was built in 1772 to make possible the founding of the New Town to the north : it was continued a few years later with the South Bridge, carrying the road across the Cowgate. To the west, the George IV Bridge was constructed between 1827 and 1836, leading from the Mound across the foot of the Lawnmarket by a second higher level street over the Cowgate. These thoroughfares effectively breached the single-street layout and relieved the ancient congestion.

Between them stand St. Giles (30), the old Parliament House (30) now incorporated in the Law Courts, the renewed Mercat Cross (52), and the present Council Chambers, once the Royal Exchange (52). Here also is the site of the Tolbooth, against which stood the enclosed, superior shops, the Luckenbooths, which, with the krames, the wooden booths erected against the buttresses of St. Giles after the Reformation, made the airt a shopping centre. In building the krames, the Kirk was treated with little respect ; mouldings and string-courses were cut away as it suited the tenants. Some attempt was originally made to maintain a high level of trading by a Council edict that only goldsmiths, jewellers, watchmakers, and booksellers should occupy the Kirk precincts. But by 1829 when the whole lot were swept away, the booths had come to sell chiefly toys and sweeties, shoes and old clothes : old and queer and cheap, they were the delight of children. Unfortunately, the process of tidying-up St. Giles went much further, and the last state of the Kirk left it far worse than it had ever been.

William Burn was one of those architects who in his youth built very creditably in the classical style—as witness the fine parish church of North Leith—but who made the classical approach to Gothic with fatal results. The Crown steeple, that gracefully and lightly rides above Edinburgh, is an example of a restoration made in the earlier seventeenth century, under one of the Milnes ; a faithful recapitulation of the fifteenth century original achieved by masons for whom the Gothic tradition was not yet dead, as can be seen by original works of that period, notably some of the Fife kirk towers. But by 1829 the whole concept of ornamental masonry had changed, and Burn could brazenly reface St. Giles with paving-stones that have no structural meaning, some of them actually resting their joints on the points of the windows. He could scrap Norman and Gothic work, doorways and tracery and whole chapels, for his own misconceptions, and construct elaborate sterile niches purposely intended to be left forever empty. It was a period of play-acting. Burn was by no means the vilest of them, there were worse to follow : some of his original work, such as the House of Falkland, has a Castle of Otranto richness to its deliberate fantasy. Even St. John's Church in Princes Street is not without its points (if indeed it has not rather too many). But in St. Giles he came to something that had been peculiarly splendid, in the way of real and inspired creation, and left it a silly toy. Only, from a distance, its proportions retain a certain dignity, and the crown steeple he mercifully left undesecrated, it is said for lack of funds.

The lantern of the crown steeple is formed of eight flying buttresses meeting to support the central pinnacle and supported by eight pinnacled buttresses rising from the corners and sides of the square tower. Below, there are triple round-headed windows, and below again, pointed windows. There is a sweet quality to the masonry in marked contrast to the hard lines of Burn's work. It is a Gothic development almost peculiar to Scotland. King's College in Aberdeen has one, also renovated at an early period, and all three capitals of Lothian were once graced with crown steeples. That at Haddington fell down under the

41   St. Bernard's Well by the Water of Leith

From the print by W. L. Leitch (1854)

period of extreme neglect of churches after the Reformation. That at Linlithgow was wantonly dismantled in the early nineteenth century. The only English example is the fine steeple at Newcastle.

The 1829 improvements became quickly a source of shame, and they were followed fifty years later by alterations conducted with more discrimination under the advice of William Chambers. Since the Reformation St. Giles had been divided, at various times, to provide a number of premises for different preachers. By 1829 it comprised the High Kirk to the east, the Old Kirk in the centre, the Tolbooth Kirk and Haddo's Hole to the west. It also contained the Assembly meeting-place in the Preston Aisle, and the Police Offices in the north transept. Haddo's Hole, less commonly known as the Little Kirk, is supposed to have received its name from a gallant cavalier supporter of Charles I, Sir John Gordon of Haddo, who was imprisoned there by the Covenanters before his execution at the Mercat Cross : but there is evidence that the name is earlier. The last of the partitions was removed in 1878, leaving the interior much as it is to-day except for the chapel for the Knights of the Thistle who had lacked this amenity since the desecration of the Holyrood Church under William of Orange. But a church built for a high altar, with side chapels, can hardly be happily adapted for pulpit-worship, and the interior remains regrettably depressing, cluttered with seats in apparent chaos, with no form, focus, or clearly comprehended function, all presided over by a vast kist of whistles.

St. Giles churchyard originally ran right down the slope to the south. After the Reformation it became increasingly encroached upon, until to-day it retains only one known tomb. It is a tomb graced by the finest statue in Edinburgh, inappropriately it is John Knox's tomb, and still more inappropriately (or is it indeed with a sweet justice ?) the figure is not that of the irate reformer but of Mary's merriest great-grandson, Charles II. There is a stone nearby engraved I. K. 1592, but as far as it is possible to determine Knox's last resting-place it is precisely under the present site of the monument to Charles, a man for all his faults far less lacking in Christianity, and a greater benefactor to Edinburgh even if he did no more than complete the Palace of Holyroodhouse.

III

The Parliament Close (53), that pavement between St. Giles and the amiable if undistinguished façade of Sir Robert Reid's Law Courts, is a pleasant place, with Charles's charger trampling its pedestal between the grey stone walls. But, vastly preferable as Reid's work is to Burn's, being candidly classical, it also refaced and defaced a better. The old front of the Parliament House was a luscious assemblage of turret and moulded details, the blazons and enriched casements of the last careless phase of unserious fortification. And little enough is left of Scottish Jacobean architecture.

It was begun in 1632 and finished seven years later. Until that time the Scottish Parliaments had been meeting, along with the Law Courts and the Town Council of Edinburgh, in the more solid and formidable but incommodious Tolbooth. There was bitter feeling that Charles I did not himself condescend to attend the opening. Of all the Stewarts, Charles I was the least considerate of Scotland. Whatever he may have meant to England, in Scotland he chiefly provoked needless discord and narrowness, although he had the support of some of the noblest characters in the country. The Covenanters who rose against him were as brave as he, and as thrawn and opinionated : they often lacked, however, his grace and bearing in dying. Many were condemned and cruelly tortured in the Laigh Parliament House itself, the vaults beneath the Hall, now an annexe of the National Library. Courageous they certainly were, but they customarily shouted and reviled their judges, damning them to hellfire in a spirit Knoxian rather than Christian, so that there is something pathetic rather than sublime about many of the martyrs of the Covenant. They had forgotten the revealing words of Paul that express that unique demand made upon the Christian martyr : " If I give my body to be burned, but have not charity, it profiteth me nothing."

Besides the Laigh Parliament House a good deal of the old roof remains, with its corner turrets, although screened from the ground by the classical façade. The Great Hall itself is almost unchanged beneath its deep hammer-beam ceiling. Here from its building until the last clamant debates of 1707 the Scottish Parliament met. It was a single chamber house, comprising the Three Estates : the Lords, the representatives of the country, and the representatives of the burghs.

The Union debates were violently contested, and followed by the whole population of Edinburgh at a pitch of great excitement. For a Scotsman it is impossible not to think of the occasion with shame : and to an Englishman it can only be remembered with an amused appreciation at his own countrymen putting a fast one across a neighbouring nation. The humiliating and for long impoverishing terms of the Treaty could only be lubricated

43 The University to-day

42 The University, about 1840

44 The Edinburgh
Volunteer, 1791

45   The City Tron Men :
Chimney-sweepers of *c.* 1795

46   " This represents old Geordy
Sime,
A famous piper in his
time " (1798)

47   Samuel MacDonald of the
Sutherland Fencibles (1790)

48 " The Evening
Walk " (1790)

49 The Lord Provost of 1815:
Sir John Marjoribanks, Bt.

50 " Military Promenade " (1795) : a skit on fashions.

From John Kay's " Original Portraits and Caricatures " (1837)

51 The Castle and Old Town after the building of Adam's North Bridge. *From a print by Ph. Mercier* (1781)

through the Edinburgh Parliament by copious bribes. Scotland had already been impoverished by the Union of the Crowns: English enmity with France damaged her ancient trade with that country, and the English merchants were jealous of Scottish competition in the trade with the Low Countries which they considered their own perquisite. Few of the Scottish peers could afford the state visits to London that became necessary for the conduct of the nation's affairs. But the acceptance of the humiliating terms offered in the Treaty were quite simply and literally a selling of their country. Lord Banff betrayed the cheapest conscience by accepting £11, 2s. as the price of his vote, even the Provost of Wigtown expected £25. At the opposite end of the scale the Duke of Queensberry, as Lord High Commissioner, set his price at £12,325.

Far beyond the Capital indignation seethed. One Finlay, an ex-sergeant of the Royal Scots, led a band from Glasgow in ill-armed protest, but was quickly gaoled in the Castle. That remarkable and far-sighted man, Andrew Fletcher of Saltoun, friend of Rousseau and a strong republican, made a series of political speeches exceptional for their integrity, in which he advocated a federal as opposed to an incorporating union. George Lockhart of Carnwath was spokesman for the Jacobite and Episcopalian faction, which was strong in its opposition: his *Memorials* are excellent literature, in the Clarendon tradition of tempered and balanced statement achieving unqualified emphasis. Lord Belhaven made ornate speeches that sometimes entangled him in his own rhetoric. The Duke of Hamilton, with one eye upon his own chances of the Throne, played a double game that eventually discomfited the opposition. The Act at last was signed, partly in a cellar in the High Street and partly in an arbour at the back of Moray House to escape from the furious mob that filled the Royal Mile crying death to the signatories. " The end of an auld sang," said Chancellor Seafield, and Queensberry fled to England during the night with the Treaty.

Undoubtedly the initial effects of the Union upon Scotland were devastating. Robert Chambers describes the next fifty years as the City's " dark age." Everything declined. Poverty became acute, leading to fierce riots. Although bright sparks gathered about Allan Ramsay's lending library in the Luckenbooths, much of the intellectual life was, like much of the wealth, lost to London. Amongst the many contemporary complaints of the state of affairs we have Ramsay's reference to the Canongate, where the representatives had been accustomed to reside, in his elegy on Lucky Wood (a keeper of good ale):

> O Cannigate ! poor elritch Hole
> What Loss, what Crosses does thou thole !
> London and Death gars thee look drole
> And hing thy Head ;
> Wow, but thou has e'en a cauld coal
> To blaw indeed.

Palace and Castle had been emptied of their life, now the Parliament House ceased to merit its name. From the flanks of St. Giles, the commercial contagion of the krames spread into the Parliament Hall itself, which became a covered market.

Sixty years ago James Grant wrote of it in *Old and New Edinburgh* : " Years of national torpor and accepted degradation followed, and to the Scot who ventured south but a sorry welcome was accorded ; yet from this state of things Scotland rose to what she is to-day, by her own exertions, unaided, and often obstructed. A return made to the House of Commons in 1710 shows that the proportion of the imperial revenue contributed by Scotland was only 2¼ per cent., whereas by the year 1866 it had risen to 14½ per cent. During that period the revenue of England increased 800 per cent., while that of Scotland increased 2,500 per cent., thus showing that there is no country in Europe which has made such vast material progress ; and to seek for a parallel case we must turn to Australia or to the United States of America. . . ."

Grant's world does not seem quite so rosy to us to-day as it did to him. We may be too hard on it, but we have tasted the bitter fruit of the decline that was actually starting in Scotland at the very time he was writing, signalised by the collapse of the City of Glasgow Bank. England's firmer-grounded, slower-matured expansion continued a while longer, and her decline has been less spectacular. We know, too, something of the cost of this material progress, both in the co-existent destitution and in the curious anarchic irresponsibility that arises in a country whose essential government is unsatisfactory. Only had it been possible for the two countries to fuse into Great Britain by the loss of their separate identities, as was the design of the Union—a process surely equally detestable to English and Scots alike—could the United Parliament have governed Scotland satisfactorily and successfully. Otherwise it had to remain what it is, an absentee government. Of course, it may be argued that the Scots are not a politically sensible people : but that is rather emphasised in contrast to the English, surely the most politically sane and sober people in the world, if, on that account, a little inclined to over-emphasise the importance of political commonsense. The French, for example, have maintained a high degree of civilisation without it.

A certain mutual antipathy, one of the great preservatives of nationhood, has prevented Great Britain from being more than a name, and one now falling into desuetude. The substantive Briton has, as someone observed, a woad-like sound : to assume it is like standing undressed in a Council Chamber (I speak with no experience of either predicament). It is, in short, a political expedient, not a human state of existence.

The phenomenon of Scottish survival is interesting, for the circumstances of her absorption are without precise parallel in the history of well-defined nationalities. There was no tyranny, as with the Irish occupation, but a venial selling-out on the part of the Scottish leaders. Then, after a period of acute distress, a singular spontaneous combustion that produced the swift, if often cruel, expansion that so impressed nineteenth century Scots with their country's vitality. Somehow the two countries did co-exist despite the intentions of an incorporating union. Somehow Edinburgh although losing almost every capital trait, Throne, Parliament, personalities, remains even now, for all her most bitter critics may say, a Capital City.

IV

Scotland did retain two institutions of her own, and of these the greatest factor in the preservation for Edinburgh of the ethos of a Capital has been not the Church but the Law. The Presbyterian Church could have maintained its headquarters in any provincial town, for its constitution is democratic, its Moderator annually elected from any part of the country. But, although the Scottish legal system is in form less centralised than the English, the Law demanded somewhere a High Court and a background for its judges and senators. The Supreme Judicature set up by James V first met in the Edinburgh Tolbooth in 1532, and moved across to the Parliament House with the Estates. The Faculty of Advocates, from whom the Judges are nominated, is a body with a distinguished record of integrity and patriotism; it is also the last actively surviving trade guild in Scotland, retaining many of its ancient powers and privileges. No better fate could have befallen the Parliament House when it lost its place as the seat of government than that it should have devolved into the home of Scottish Law. The legal fraternity from thenceforward became increasingly important, gradually occupying a unique position as the centre of Scotland's intellectual life and very largely the guardians of the nation's rights and continued existence. The great Edinburgh personalities from the middle of the eighteenth to about the middle of the nineteenth centuries were practically without exception associated with the Law. It was no accident that Sir Walter Scott was a lawyer : he could hardly have been otherwise. The Profession provided the only background against which he could thrive : intellectual life had become almost identical with legal life. Boswell was a not very successful advocate : his father was a Judge. Hume became librarian to the Advocates. Jeffrey, whose criticism seemed immortal to his own generation but proved as transient as most of its genre, and Cockburn, whose *Memorials* and *Circuit Journeys* remain delightful reading, were two of the radical rebels of the turn of the century, both ending on the Bench. If such writers as Henry Mackenzie, author of *The Man of Feeling*, are never likely to be read again, they preserved interest and judgment and taste in their way. If by its nature the Law imposed certain obvious restrictions upon the literary field that it dominated, at least it was the lawyers themselves who first welcomed Burns to the Capital, and gave him the encouragement he needed.

The almost legendary figure of the old-style Scottish judge is not entirely extinct even in our own day. And now when legality, with its order and humanity, is menaced by the spreading blight of bureaucracy, it is infinitely refreshing to visit the Parliament House. Here there are no Jacks and Jills in Office to tell you from a printed form whether you are a criminal or a properly social and servile subject. Wig and gown provide a blessed unfunctional panoply where the advocates parade beneath the hammer-beams of the Corridor. Even the most wretched offender in the dock is treated like a human being—to be respected or bullied according to the mercy of his judges, but not docketed, sub-sectioned, categoried, and filed. He may be hanged, imprisoned, admonished, released : he is a man amongst men. The judge may be generous, sanctimonious, prosy, obtuse, acute, rugged, succinct : he is always a fellow man, by some mercy of Providence, not through having been properly placed in the Civil Service exams, upon this and not the other side of the Bench, striving to do justice in the knowledge that he is human and prone to error : he never sinks to the depth of trying to ape the machine.

Forbye the Advocates, there is the Society of Clerks, or Writers to His Majesty's Signet, of which a member is designated **W.S.** These have exclusive rights to certain branches of legal procedure that place them in a superior category to the S.S.C., the Solicitor before the Supreme Courts. Most of the Writers practise in Edinburgh, their brass plates glinting from the doorways of the New Town. With the Faculty, they have brought the legal profession in the City to a standard of integrity and competence that make it unique in the world to-day. The anxiety to bring a case to Court, the alarming tendency to make the Law a speculative concern, and the widespread connivance at dubious conduct that have brought the Law in London to so low a pass, are comparatively unknown in Edinburgh. About the Glasgow solicitor there is a certain *joie de vivre* and provincial gusto, but there is also a lack of a proper respect for his Profession. Nor, since Scottish Law is not case law but more strictly deriving from Roman Law, maintaining the concept of justice above precedence, has this preoccupation with legality been allowed to become case-hardened or inflexible.

In losing the Court, Edinburgh lost panoply and stimulus, if also some of its less-desirable hangers-on. In losing resident politicians, she no doubt lost a good deal of liveliness and enterprise. In replacing them as leaders of her Society with lawyers trained and proud in their Profession, she has gained in dignity and honour, elements whose value seems clearer to us in days when we see responsibility becoming sterilised as the prerogative of the State. If certain ludicrous elements of social rectitude have come to be associated with the City's life, the Edinburgh man himself does not take them so seriously, for he knows how much remains of the old convivial spirit of the *Noctes Ambrosianae*, and that the dignity of the Legal Profession would never suffer it to become teetotal. Of course the consumption is not on the old gargantuan scale (for long helped by a happy oversight whereby Scotland was enabled to purchase claret without the heavy English tariff that the Union imposed upon all her important imports). The stories of learned juridical potations related by Cockburn and others remain to us heroic legends : but the characters and deeds do not differ in kind from persons we have rejoiced to know and occasions at which we have ourselves assisted.

V

It was long before Medicine anywhere achieved the standing of the Law. It had to become considerably less of a speculative science, or venture, than it was in its beginnings. In the seventeenth century a German who came to Edinburgh to sell a very commendable specific for the stomach required the support of a juggler to attract custom, and such attractions were long associated with physic. Edinburgh, however, early showed sympathy for the young science—Sir Patrick Geddes suggested that, like Paris, she owed the supremacy of her Medical School to her insalubrious conditions providing copious material for practice. The first regular dissection in the City was made in 1694 by Dr. Alexander Pitcairn, a notable citizen who had returned from Leyden, where he held the Chair of Medicine, to get married, and was induced to stay by the Physicians. Dr. Pitcairn got his bodies from the House of Correction and the Foundling Hospital, and shortly after the College of Surgeons gained like facilities.

Dr. Pitcairn was a learned wit of a kind very necessary to the maintenance of the City's intellectual life during its " dark age," of which Robert Chambers wrote : " From the Union up to the middle of this century, the existence of the City seems to have been a perfect blank. No improvements of any sort marked the period. On the contrary an air of gloom and depression pervaded the City, such as distinguished its history at no former period. A tinge was communicated even to the manners and fashions of society, which were remarkable for stiff reserve, precise moral carriage, and a species of decorum amounting almost to morose-ness, sure indications, it is to be supposed, of a time of adversity and humiliation." Defeatism took its customary form, and people sought the hard protective carapace of puritanical Calvinism. For all its merits as preservative, it has a bad concomitant in the hypocrisy and cant that it thrusts upon innumerable weaker vessels for whom it sets a pace that it would take a saint to maintain in charity.

Dr. Pitcairn, besides his fascinating compilation of *Criminal Trials* and his many important medical papers, wrote a play called *The Assembly* which, if somewhat scurrilous, gives an interesting picture of the religious humbug of his day. He was a Jacobite and an Episcopalian, often accused of being an atheist, and maintained a continuous flippant fight with the Ministry. The Kirk Officers who were detailed to prowl the Sabbath streets for those who infringed the rigid decorum imposed, were in the habit of confiscating wine and other consumable articles carried by sabbath-breakers or their servants. Pitcairn doctored some of his wine with a violent emetic, which thenceforward preserved his goods from interference. In his Latin lyrics he warns the stranger who would learn of Edinburgh to avoid the then triple church of St. Giles :

" *Tres ubi Cyclopes fanda nefanda boant.*"

52 The Mercat Cross and Royal Exchange, now City Buildings

53   Statue of Charles II in Parliament Square

54   Conflagration of the Tron Church, 16th November 1824

55   The Lawnmarket about 1840.

From contemporary prints

and seek the sanctuaries of the rosy god, worshipped night and day in such taverns as the Cross Keys, the Ship, Buchanan's, and Tennant's where scalloped oysters were served with the wine. And he lists those more intimate dens, deep-hidden down wynds and closes, where he and his fellows were constantly to be found. " Here you may be both merry and wise, but beware how you toast kings and their French retreats." His favourite establishment was in the Pillars, one of the big buildings that stood in the Parliament Close and were destroyed in the Great Fire of 1824 : it was known as the Greping Office, and, on account of its dark entry, patrons had to grope their way into it. Here he gave consultations and frank medical advice to the poor who waited upon him as he drank and talked with his friends.

Pitcairn's play was never acted, and was I think first published in London after his death. The Theatre was firmly proscribed. In fact, it has yet to recover as a national institution. It is not too much to say that for the last play dealing pertinently and critically with Scottish life we have to go back to Sir David Lyndsay's *Satire of the Three Estaitis*, a fine work and outspoken in its criticism of the abuses in Crown, State, and the Catholic Church (of which Lyndsay remained a member). The Catholics were not so incapable of self-criticism and *The Three Estaitis* was performed before Mary of Lorraine out at Braidburn, where now, oddly enough, the Corporation has its Open-Air Theatre. James VI had a major row with the ministers when he brought Fletcher's Company up from London—a tour in which Shakespeare may well have appeared, and on which he may subsequently have received the freedom of Aberdeen bestowed upon the Company by an appreciative magistracy adequately remote from the influence of Knox. There are occasional references to visiting companies in Edinburgh after that time, and to the measures taken by the Kirk to eject them. James VII created scandal by his plays in the tennis court at Holyrood, and from then on there was virtually no play-acting, outside the pulpit, until in 1738 Allan Ramsay opened his theatre in Carrubber's Close. It was Ramsay's only failure, being immediately closed down by order of the magistrates under duress of the Kirk, and the hopes of a Scottish drama died for another long age.

It all countries it was a bad age for the expositors of religion. The common cleric was customarily poor and ignorant. Although, as a whole, the Scottish clergy were perhaps better placed than those of many countries, an example of elementary ignorance upon the subject of mortal sin is provided by the case of the Reverend Daniel MacLachlan who, in 1735, wrote a perfectly serious pamphlet, and caused it to be printed in London, under the uncompromising title : *An Essay upon Improving and Adding to the Strength of Great Britain and Ireland by Fornication.* Presumably the pragmatic approach justified for Mr. MacLachlan the vice that was the particular object of the attentions of that sordid institution, the Session Courts, whose operations led to plentiful abuse of the type retailed by Allan Ramsay in his Elegy upon an Edinburgh Session Clerk. The fact that Ramsay could write and sell such verses shows the persistence of a healthy criticism, although, plainly, the rift was too deeply marked, and letters too sharply divided into what was at worst, and almost invariably, the pedantic and sanctimonious on the one hand, and the topically scurrilous on the other. As we have remarked, the times were too dark for an abiding literature to come out of Edinburgh.

The earliest Scottish printing had been under charter from James IV granted to Andrew Millar and Walter Chepman. Millar was a merchant in Edinburgh and Chepman seems to have learnt the craft at Rouen. Chaucer was the first author chosen, in 1508, and the following year saw the publication of the first volume of Bishop Elphinstone's *Aberdeen Breviary.* It is probable that the enlightened founder of King's College had much to do with the introduction of a press into Scotland. In a recent paper on typography given in Edinburgh, Mr. Stanley Morison stressed how disastrous an effect the Reformation had taken upon the art, since from then until the eighteenth century " its value consisted solely in its economic and propagandist usefulness." Bassandyne's Bible, printed in the High Street with imported types, is an exception, a very competent piece of work, as is the Prayer Book of Charles I that raised so much stour.

The centre of the book trade that developed in the eighteenth century lay in the neighbourhood of the Luckenbooths, where Allan Ramsay opened his lending library in 1725. Wodrow, the Calvinist, protested violently against these " villainous, profane, and obscene books," but the library survived to contain some 30,000 volumes and be the great delight of Walter Scott's boyhood. The trade in later years so flourished in Edinburgh that there was a series of attempts on the part of the London booksellers to put a close to it. Vigorous action finally established the legal position in Edinburgh's favour, and to this day the City retains the highest book sales per head of population of any in the world.

When Ramsay sold his business it passed through the hands of James MacEwan and Alexander Kincaid, men of note in their time, finally becoming the property of William Creech, who for forty-four years made the shop in the Luckenbooths (stone-built, close to the north side of the choir of St. Giles), with its books and its coffee-room, the chief centre of intellectual exchange. He published two literary periodicals, the *Mirror* and the *Lounger*, besides the books of nearly all the leading Scottish writers of his day, including Burns, Adam Smith, and Dr. Gregory of the powder, and the works of the great lawyers. He was a man of parts, but was deemed tight-fisted and lacking in the enterprise shown by his successors, Constable and the Blackwoods, who indeed were able to capture many of the English authors in the early nineteenth century.

VI

Post-Reformation Edinburgh had three memorably destructive fires, and each of them was in the central region of the Parliament Close. The first, in 1700, destroyed the highest tenements in the town, those that were said to have risen up to fourteen storeys from the south at the Kirkheugh, the Scottish Treasury Room, the Exchequer and Exchange. These included " all the statelie buildings of Thomas Robertson," a seventeenth-century specu-lative builder whose transactions and eventual bankruptcy have recently been described for the Old Edinburgh Club by Dr. Marguerite Wood, Keeper of the City Records, and provide some interesting sidelights upon their day. The Exchange in particular must have been *statelie*, and it is unfortunate that no picture of it exists. It was designed by Sir William Bruce, with " carved work upon the entrie," black-and-white marble paving, and " extraordinary work upon the pillars and severall other pairts of the samyn." There seems to have been a passage of perhaps fifty goodly shops running through it, rented at from £36 to £48 Scots a year, and selling at up to sixteen years' purchase. Robert-son's own tenement in the Close itself had a " scale and platt stair : " *i.e.* a straight stairway broken by landings, which was a new fangle, considered more refined than the old turnpike. It is perhaps worth remarking that in fact the discredited turnpike has much to recommend it. Contrary to popular belief, it is a safer design, since one cannot fall very far down it without reaching the wall, it being impossible to fall in a spiral. It has great charm, both within and as an exterior projection, is architectually con-venient and adaptable, is fireproof, and to-day the components can readily be constructed with a concrete mould.

The fire was naturally regarded as a judgment upon the vices of the lax. And even the two great fires of 1824 were stigmatised in a sermon and a pamphlet by a Doctor of Divinity as being directly intended by the Almighty as a sharp riposte to the City for countenancing a Musical Festival. Such was the nervous and unspiritual irrationality of pragmatic Presbyterianism : but indeed it has ever been the delight of the moraliser to invest God or Fate with his own meanness of spirit.

After the 1700 fire the rebuilding of the Parliament Close had been carried out in a uniform style in accordance with a Burgh decree of 1698, interesting as an early application of a renewal in urban planning. They were considered the best building carried out in the City from that day until the opening of the New Town. Although not so high as their predecessors they were substantial erections, standing as they did in the valuable heart of the City, rising to about 130 feet from the lower level. They were all destroyed in the two fires of June and November, 1824. The first started in one of the open-all-night spirit cellars at the head of the Royal Bank Close, gutting the whole of the east side of the Parliament Close. The second was even more devastating. It destroyed the Old Assembly Rooms and many of the old lands, besides the remainder of the Parliament Close. It took place on two November nights : and in fact the second conflagration was considered to have had an independent origin, except for an independent flare-up of the steeple of the Tron Kirk (54), where probably sparks from the night before had smouldered to burst at last into flames. The excitement was very great indeed, with the vast height of the buildings, their wild blaze little checked by the efforts of totally inadequate fire engines.

Although by modern standards the loss of life was negligible, the loss of property was considerable. Each time the Law Courts were threatened, but were saved. The Tron Kirk spire, which was a charming piece of seventeenth century work was replaced by the present monstrosity, which dwarfs and makes inconspicuous the abbreviated little church behind it so that it looks like a grubby little boy skulking behind the skirts of an overdressed and unpleasant mamma. The Tron, after which this early post-Reformation church, one of the works of John Milne, was named, was the public weigh-house which stood forenenst it a little way down from the Mercat Cross.

The present Mercat Cross (52) is a Victorian replacement of the original, and is of small interest save as showing how the style of burgh crosses developed in the bigger towns of Scotland. It has a drum, through which the platform is reached. Part of the cross shaft is a relic of the old cross, which was of far more pleasing proportion and decoration. It was itself an early seventeenth century renovation of a still earlier cross.

From the Cross the Royal Proclamations were read, including that of Prince Charles in September, 1745. It was also the superior place of execution, where Kirkaldy of Grange was basely hanged, with his face turned to the sun, and where Montrose was hanged, and the Regent Morton and the Argyles were beheaded. One of the only Scottish priests to be killed at the Reformation, Sir James Tarbat, was stoned to death at the Cross, or as Knox describes it, served with " his Easter eggs." Eleven MacGregor caterans finished a life of raiding along Lochlomondside by swinging on the gibbet at the Cross in 1636. Their leader was the red-haired lad, *an Ghille Ruadh*, whose Gaelic name became pleasantly romanced into Gilderoy, and he the subject of an Edinburgh street ballad, put into the mouth of his mistress :

> My love he was as brave a man
> As ever Scotland bred,
> Descended from a Highland clan,
> A catheran to his trade.
> No woman then or womankind
> Had ever greater joy
> Than we two when we lived alone,
> I and my Gilderoy.

On the north side of the roadway from the Cross, set back behind a forecourt, is the building (52) that after long delay replaced Bruce's Royal Exchange. It was not completed until 1761. It backs on to what is now Cockburn Street, whence it shows one of the most impressive cliffs of masonry left, notably well built and rising a hundred feet. The front is of more modest proportion, an effective piece of arcaded classical design, with four Corinthian pilasters supporting a pediment mounting the City arms. As an Exchange it was never a great success, the merchants preferring to do their business in the street in the old manner. But early in the last century the Town Council obtained accommodation in the building, which is now the Council Chambers.

Some interesting old houses adjacent were recently demolished to expand the Chambers, and to-day there is little in the airt interesting in the way of domestic architecture. One block worth noting stands farther down on the same side, a six storey tenement of the eighteenth century, remarkable for the way in which lavish fenestration in no sense weakens the sense of bield and solidity, a straightforward frontage executed with a lovely sense of proportion. In Hunter Square, back of the Tron Kirk, the old Merchants' Hall has a particularly charming classical front, and some good interior detail, while its back seen from Stevenlaw's Close, retains, with its stair projection, the imposing ruggedness of the earlier fabrics. The Hall was deserted by the merchants for premises in the New Town, the Hanover Street offices of the unfortunate City of Glasgow Bank, and a bank has taken over the old Hall and stupidly spoilt the lower part of the front with conventional banker's pomposity.

Despite the way in which its best buildings have been sullied by conceited improvements, this short stretch of the High Street must always seem the essence of the Edinburgher's Edinburgh. That godly crown of St. Giles has arrested us in our late-night step, after drinking and arguing in wealth of words, rambling through letters and metaphysics, through politics to the more heartening hopes of the nation : those plans for Scotland made without fear of the disillusionment of success in our time. We have hurled High Toryism and Whiggery, the hard narking materialism of Marxism, and sheer high spirits into the melting-pot of the evening, and the company has grown in the bars and then strangely dwindled till only two found their way to drink coffee in this airt beneath the Crown steeple. Still our voices were loud, and then we came out into the dark High Street beneath the steeple, and quietness gained of that sense, suddenly realised, of being part of so ancient a tradition. Not steps to heaven or hell, but something offthrown, an ingenious patterning that we wear, but can slough like a snakeskin. We take our place unseen in the pageant of a City's life, a life independent of ours, and yet for a blissful moment resting upon us.

Or the Law brings us more awesomely to this quarter, or, more light-heartedly, a wedding in a chapel of the High Kirk. And I remember some remarkable interviews with the most provostly Provost of recent times, his lum-hatted head set against a sunlit city spread out far below the high back of the Council Chambers like an ancient map in semi-perspective. The major-domo with his red-facings serving us with the City's sherry, and the talks achieving nothing but a merry glint in the memory. On New Year's eve the Tron Kirk besieged by a suitably seething and unreckoning crowd ; the clock striking, and an eightsome reel danced in eminent and distinguished company eminently contented to be indistinct.

Old Town and Canongate

I

NORTH AND SOUTH, THE STREETS OF THE BRIDGES MEET WHERE
their line intersects the High Street, and are now the more
emphatic thoroughfare, with their tramlines and through
traffic. Compared with them the High Steeet is sluggish and
amiable, with knots of neighbours talking together as they have
always done. The slope of the Royal Mile grows steeper beyond
the Bridges. Almost immediately, on the right, Niddry Street
has replaced the historic Niddry's Wynd, descending sharply
to the Cowgate. The line of the Wynd lay a little farther west,
but one of its old buildings, and that perhaps the most interesting
of all, still stands in the street, into which it abuts, having been
set back from the wynd. We see it now as a gaudy dance hall,
but its eighteenth century lineaments remain to testify to its
original more fragrant association with a sister muse.

It is the old St. Cecilia's Hall, musically the most historic
building in Scotland. It was an early fruit of the vitality that
returned to Edinburgh half-way through the eighteenth century.
Up till that time public musical entertainment had been confined
to one or two taverns, notably Steil's near the Parliament Close,
where the intelligentsia foregathered, and Dr. Pitcairn met with
his intimate but more political friend, Fletcher of Saltoun. Music
was of course under the ban of the Kirk, and had to seek hospitality
amongst the outlaws. But with the growth of confidence and so
of opposition amongst more generous minds, the Musical Society
was able to build itself the lovely little hall with its entry from
Niddry's Wynd.

Although the plan of the hall is now oblong, the oval glass
cupola remains to indicate its former internal design, and to give
a distinction surprising to its present tawdry. It was the last
Edinburgh work of the Milne family, of that Robert Milne who
later went to London but in 1762 had newly returned to Edinburgh from Rome, where he had won " the first prize in the first
class of architecture." He based his design upon the great opera

61

house of Parma : the acoustics and seating arrangements were notably good, and there was a space in front of the orchestra for a promenade during the intervals. About four hundred could be seated. The Niddry's Wynd entrance is now flattened by the removal of its portico for the passage of the street. The Cowgate entrance, dated 1812, belongs to a later phase of the building's varied history, the time when it was the Masonic Hall. It remains one of the most deserving of the City's many old misused structures. It would take very little to convert it again into a concert hall, or even a small theatre, and it remains conveniently central.

St. Cecilia's was the weekly resort of the later eighteenth century aristocracy. It was for a time the chief place of social intercourse, and many remarkable personalities attended its concerts. Fiddler Tam, the Jacobite sixth Earl of Kelly, Pitcairn's grandson, was a considerable musician amongst the patrons. He composed and played symphonies, overtures, and songs. That excellent worthy and amateur, George Thomson, the collector of the *Melodies of Scotland* and collaborator with Burns, was a main prop of the Society. He was, of course, a lawyer by profession. To him we owe the preservation of many traditional airs, and their harmonising by Beethoven, Haydn, Kozeluch, and others. He was a fervent supporter of the works of Haydn against the intransigeant Handelians. The great beauties of the age, Miss Burnet of Monboddo, Miss Betsy Home, Miss Murray of Lintrose, Miss Hay of Hayston, and Jane, Duchess of Gordon (who as a High Street lassie was seen riding on the back of a pig belonging to a neighbouring publican) were amongst the regular attractions. It was a custom with the gallants to repair after the concerts to Fortune's Tavern where challenges were drunk in tribute to rival beauties. He who drank deepest was said to have " saved " his lady even if he floored himself.

Of the many Continental performers who appeared at St. Cecilia's, some of whom, like the Corris, settled in Edinburgh, the greatest was Tenducci, for whom his friend Mozart wrote a song. Tenducci seems to have been a magnificent singer, and a fine generous personality. He brought "Gilderoy" out of its background in the street beyond into the refinement of St. Cecilia's, and sang it along with other Scottish songs together with his classical repertoire. The great Italian's rendering of these songs created a tremendous impression and directly inspired the compilation of the *Melodies of Scotland.* This appreciation of the native airs, according them, as it were, a social status, prepared the way for the appreciation of Burns in the Capital.

Tenducci has another indirect but pertinent association with

62

56   The West Bow from the Grassmarket

57   Bakehouse Close

Burns, for he befriended a mad genius of a halfling, Robert Fergusson, a medical student who, driven almost demented by his study of diseases, had to give up medicine for the greater consolation of the High Street howffs and the writing of his poetry.

Fergusson is a significant figure amongst Scottish poets. The linguistic difficulty that faced our poets after the Reformation cannot easily be overestimated. In pre-Reformation days the Court poets, Dunbar and Lyndesay, and the ecclesiastics, Henryson and Bishop Gavin Douglas, wrote in the Scots dialect. Knox, who had long been out of Scotland, was twitted by Nicholas Winyet for " knapping suddrons " (as it might be : " talking Cockney ") and with having forgotten his mother tongue. His introduction of an English Bible was, of course, a deathly blow to the native language. Hence a real difficulty for the poets who followed : the gradual divorce of the written tongue from that still generally spoken (stimulating, of course, the breaking up of the latter into various dialects). It was easiest for such cavaliers as Drummond of Hawthornden, with English associations, to use English for their writings, and the ballad-makers, whose work was passed on orally and was never written down till far later, could stick to their spoken tongue. But, added to the general antipathy of the Kirk to the arts, the rift between writing and speaking made a serious practical difficulty for poets, as is illustrated in the peculiar lameness of the majority of Scottish eighteenth century versifiers writing in English. It was not merely that this was an age of formal diction, but to them the words of the convention were altogether remote from their experience.

The work of a handful of poets writing in Scots during the period following the Reformation remains, besides the anonymous pieces, to suggest a potentially vigorous survival : most notable is that single exquisite surviving sonnet of Mark Alexander Boyd. Allan Ramsay, who began life as a wig-maker, took up the thread of dialect writing again, but his verse is not remarkable. Fergusson never made any effort to express himself in literary English, but with a notable spontaneity utters' the words of the Edinburgh folk of his day, and uses them to considerable effect and with an expressive fluency of metre. Burns was emphatic in his homage to the poet whose freshness had inspired him.

When in 1769 Tenducci appeared in Arne's opera, *Artaxerxes*, in the Theatre Royal, newly opened just across the North Bridge, Robert Fergusson contributed three songs to traditional airs. The poor poet and the large, handsome, successful Italian, both generous creatures open to the dunts of the world, made warm friendship, and tears would come to the emotional Tenducci's eyes when, after Fergusson's death, his name was mentioned. Fergusson took his own life in 1774, when he was twenty-four. He was in the madhouse at the time : he had written, " The mind's ay cradled whan the grave is near."

Tenducci has also an association with Tobias Smollett. They were debtor prisoners together in the King's Bench, became friends, and Smollett, on his own release, settled with the Italian's creditors. It is related that a douce lady relative of Smollett subsequently introduced to Tenducci in Edinburgh was overcome by the warmth of the embrace with which he expressed his appreciation.

St. Cecilia's Hall was at the height of its glory about the time of Burns's visit in 1786, and he has recorded his appreciation of many of those of its patrons " whose lovely faces at the concerts gave us the sweetest zest for music " as George Thomson recalled years afterwards. George Thomson lived to be ninety-three, by which time the New Town had lured most of the high life from the Old, and St. Cecilia's was a school before declining into a warehouse.

The impact of Burns upon Edinburgh is a singular page in the Capital's history. It is a story easily romanticised. It can to-day be painted as the arrival of an honest rustic of genius upon an effete and mannered aristocracy, as easily as it was rendered in Victorian times as a *tour de force* of condescension on the part of the elite. In fact, the Edinburgh aristocracy was a robust one, little conscious of condescension, and Burns a poet and a man of great personal charm whose honest impetuosity left revealed his own human sillinesses in a way that a lesser personality could not have borne. If it made him write some very bad verses (" *Edina*, Scotia's darling seat " has been aptly commercialised by a firm of plumbers in the City), it gave him some intensely necessary encouragement, and deepened his experience, if in some ways sadly. Moreover, he did not stay to play the pet, but went back to the hard darg. While to Edinburgh his coming served as a recall to native idioms at a time when the revived culture was becoming over-dependent upon imported airs and graces.

II

Almost opposite Niddry's Wynd stood Allan Ramsay's original shop in a fine timber-fronted land. At the Sign of the Moor's Head he published his poems on penny sheets until his success took him to the Luckenbooths. Hither the bairns were sent to buy " Allan Ramsay's latest piece." He then issued his collection of Scots and English songs, *The Tea-Table Miscellany*, which the people, so long starved of secular literature, bought to the tune of twelve editions, encouraging him to produce *The Evergreen*, an unscholarly edition of ancient poetry chiefly from the Bannatyne MS. which particularly scandalised the ministers and the servile magistracy.

Ramsay's shop has been demolished, as has Archibald Constable's nearby. Constable made a great name for himself and the repute of having been the best of all Edinburgh publishers. He was said to have " total want of that critical jabber of which most of his brethren are so profuse," and he offered unprecedented fees to his authors. As much as twenty guineas a sheet for a criticism in the *Edinburgh Review*: £3000 for an epic poem : and £1000 each for two philosophical dissertations prefixed to a supplement to the first edition of the *Encyclopedia Britannica*. Small wonder that authors have revered his memory. Of his collapse in 1826, involving Sir Walter Scott, Cockburn observes : " If an earthquake had swallowed half the town, it would not have produced greater astonishment, sorrow, or dismay. Ballantyne and Constable were merchants, and their fall, had it reached no further, might have been lamented merely as the casualty of commerce. But Sir Walter ! The idea that his practical sense had so far left him as to have permitted him to dabble in trade, had never crossed our imagination."

At the same period on the opposite side of the High Street was the publishing shop of Manners and Miller. Very unlike Constable's business-like premises, it was considered excessively dandified, the blue-stocking haunt, with its exquisite bindings and paintings by Turner. Only one of the old firms remains in the airt. This is Oliver & Boyd in Tweeddale Court, the town house of the Yester family. A modest but handsome frontage of early seventeenth century character, although bearing the date 1572, it stands back in what were once its own grounds garnished with an avenue of lime trees. It became the head office of the British Linen Bank, and in the close a cashier was murdered and robbed in 1806—a crime never satisfactorily solved and long a subject of enjoyable speculation. Thereafter the Bank moved to St. Andrew Square, and the premises became the offices of the printers and publishers who still occupy them.

The next street through to the Cowgate from Niddry Street is Blackfriars Street, also the successor to a famous wynd, once long a stronghold of the dissentient elements of Episcopacy and Catholicism. The wynd was once rich in fine and historic buildings, including Cardinal Beaton's Palace, of which it now retains only two. The first is the battered remnant of the house of the Regent Morton, one of Mary's principal accusers, a man to whom it made no odds whether he was coining bad money or arranging the death of the husband of one of his mistresses. Its round stair tower projects into the street, with a good ogival doorway. It has been a timbered house, which partially accounts for its present shorn and forlorn appearance. The second stands a little farther down, and is not properly in the street, although now approached by it. Despite additions, it is still a good example of a seventeenth century house on the L plan, with an octagonal stair-tower in the re-entrant angle, and pedimented dormer windows with ball finials. It became an Industrial School shortly after the original Ragged School founded a hundred years ago by Dr. Guthrie in Ramsay Gardens for the wretched half-vagrant children with which the Old Town teemed during the Industrial Revolution.

Although Edinburgh suffered in some ways less from the evils of that time than the cities whose expansion was more sudden and mushroom-like, she had her share of them. The swift, enormous increase of population, the trekking into cities already over-crowded, the innumerable sweat-shops of the boom, brought social evils of a kind that even a more benevolent humanity could not immediately have alleviated. It is too easy to condemn the " haves " of that time, forgetting that they were faced with new problems of administration, the need to adapt to unexpected and unpredictable movements that had changed the balance of their society with the increment of a disproportionate number of persons living on the edge of destitution. The Irish famines alone brought thousands of penniless unfortunates into Edinburgh. The artisan turned by the power of the machine into a considerable employer of labour had no tradition of responsibility for the welfare of dependents : he was liable to be every bit as bad as the landlord who was coming to regard his estates as an investment instead of a responsibility. But in the Kirk a new and revolutionary genera-tion of ministers was arising, men of the humane stamp of Dr. Guthrie and Dr. Chalmers.

A warm tribute to Guthrie's schools appears in two books of reminiscences written by an Edinburgh detective of the period. Mr. MacLevy, the author, throws a unique sidelight upon this period of the City's history : intrinsically more informative than the shocking but bald and statistical accounts prepared for the Corporation by its officers of health, with their tales of almost incredible overcrowding and lack of sanitation.

It is a curious world that MacLevy pictures, where grand and beautiful houses had declined, quite quickly, into festering stews, dank with destitution and fearful with ignorance. The gaiety is of that breakneck thieving kind : a gamble to bring either a bout of whisky and women, or transportation into the unknown world of the aborigines. There is little mercy, other than the occasional grim smile that MacLevy bestows upon his captives. " You know I never had a chance ! " cries his victim. " Yes, I know. I knew your father, and that old Jezebel, your mother." " Why do you do it ? " " Just because it is my trade." And the unfortunate goes quietly, ahead of him the nightmare life of the penal settlement. Or MacLevy, an Irishman himself, arrests a handsome colleen of a hawker in the Irish Cowgate at her wedding feast, tracing her through a stolen sprig of orange blossom. " ' I choose to claim this young woman for my bride,' I said, with a little of an inward chuckle. . . . ' All of you leave the room . . . .' The girl received the last look of her departing bridegroom with the same cold indifference she had exhibited all through the strange scene. I do not say she did not feel. It is hardly possible to suppose that a young woman dressed for marriage, and in the hands of the police, with banishment before and shame behind, could be unmoved, but the mind of these creatures is so peculiarly formed that they make none of Nature's signs, and are utterly beyond our knowledge . . . they themselves have no words and no symbols. . . ." And Mr. MacLevy goes on to record his disappointment that the stolen bride would not respond to his suggestion that she should give him a stirrup cup before he led her away.

MacLevy's tales convey the strange sparking of humanity against a reversion towards drumlie animalism : a low-ceilinged life, degraded but not beyond moments of tragedy and of generosity of spirit, persisting, and heroic when seen against its background. His thieves' jargon is interesting : an old lag is an *old leg*, in reference to leg-irons : a ponce is a *pounce*, a prostitute's bully : the street-walkers are *nightingales*. He gives graphic pictures of the lands in their degeneration. In Leith Wynd at the head of the Canongate (now perjinkly called Cranston Street after a Bailie of the Burgh) there were two particularly notorious brothels and thieves' kitchens, very ancient, rambling mansions, known familiarly as the Happy Land and the Holy Land. He records a definite improvement as a result of Guthrie's innovation of the industrial school. Whatever such institutions may have become later, at that time they were havens of hope for thousands of waifs, and in their insistence upon instilling a religious sense of individual responsibility were far more realistic and valuable than their progressive counterparts of to-day. The shrewd, practical MacLevy could vouch for their marked effect in lightening his labours.

III

In Carrubber's Close is Old St. Paul's, where the episcopal congregation went to worship after being ousted from their short-lived Cathedral of St. Giles by the presbyterian party. Across the way, facing the Cowgate and approached from South Gray's Close, was the rival establishment, the Hanoverian Church. For the Scottish Episcopalians were staunch Jacobites, and in fact the handful of conforming, Hanoverian churches, were rather in the position of dissenters, celebrating the English rite, praying for his Hanoverian Majesty, and protected from many of the penalties of dissension from the Kirk. They were ultimately absorbed by their brethren when with the death of Prince Charles in 1788 the political reason for their existence had lapsed. Their church is now St. Patrick's Catholic Church, having been sold when they had built themselves the Gothic St. Paul's in the New Town, and passing first to the United Seceders and then, in 1856, to the Catholics. It dates from 1771, but was never finished until the dignified south front was recently added. It contains some paintings by one of the brothers Runciman, creditable Edinburgh painters of their school.

Down Chalmers Close stands the pathetic remnant of the Trinity College Church of Mary of Gueldres, once standing amongst delightful almshouses at the tip of the Nor' Loch where are now the sidings of the Waverley Station. It was impiously removed on a promise of re-erection, but the railway company avoided its obligations until many of the stones had been stolen from their casual storage on the Calton Hill. Thereafter, and after the inevitable litigation and quarrels, the nave was re-erected as a kind of annexe to a dull little kirk to which it brings some disused glory—lofty and subtle and devotional. It now goes by the muckle mouthful " Trinity College and Moray-Knox Church," having absorbed the congregations of two United Free and one United Presbyterian Church.

Above it, in the High Street, stand the pleasant group formed by Moubray House and John Knox's House. John Knox's House (61, 62) retains the last elaborate timber galleries in Edinburgh. Although the woodwork has had to be renewed it repeats the original work, and the whole remains the least-changed example of an Edinburgh house of Queen Mary's time. It was built by her

58 Calton Hill, with the Royal High School at its foot

59 Whitehorse Close, Canongate, about 1856

60 The old mansion house of Easter Coates

goldsmith, James Mossman, whose initials it bears, with the name of the Deity in Latin, Greek, and Scots, on a sun with rays : also the text *Lufe.God.abufe.al.and.yi.nyghbour.as.yi.self.*

Fortunately the property was at one time in the possession of one of the name of Knox, and the illusion springing up that John Knox himself had actually lived in the house, it escaped the fate of the majority of its kind. To-day it is a tourist shop and a museum of sorts : a little raree show of miscellaneous bric-à-brac, including some good Scots panelling and some strange Victorianisms. If it is unconvincing, and its very survival rooted in error, it is all the more proper a tribute to the man whose shrine it purports to be. Moubray House is perhaps the finer building of the two, although less elaborate. It retains a projecting plastered gable and an outside stair. It is the property of the Cockburn Association, who might complete their good work by replacing the astragals in the upper windows. Conspicuous and pleasant on the paving in front of these houses stands one of the six public wells left along the Royal Mile.

The end of the High Street and of old Edinburgh comes at the junction of Jeffrey Street and St. Mary's Street, the head of the Canongate and the site of the Netherbow Port (23), the finest and the last of the City's gates. A great, robust bield between its fat towers, it was demolished in 1764, having survived the last attack upon the City. In September 1745, Lochiel, Ardshiel, and Keppoch had been sent by Prince Charles with powder to blow it up to force an entry, but the gate being opened to let out the coach that had contained the deputation sent by the City to the Prince, Lochiel leapt in, wrested his musket from the sentry, and immediately was followed by his Cameron clansmen, swords drawn, pipes playing, colours flying in the moonlight.

IV

The whole story of the '45 is so fantastic that between them the glamour and its antistrophic debunking obscure an achievement that, as it concerns Scotland, if the less complete is none the less emphatic for the failure of the Prince's cause. But it is an achievement sufficiently essential in its nature to be difficult precisely to estimate. For Scotland it was very largely a nationalist movement. Although the Roman Catholics, a very small part of the community, and the Episcopalians, a more considerable element, were concerned for their own ends, they, like the vast majority

69

of the Jacobites who were, of course, Presbyterians, were at least equally concerned in avenging the moral defeat of 1707 and in gaining the freedom of their country from a union that had so far proved disastrous.

Certainly the motives that brought the Prince's army together were mixed : but in what struggle have they ever been anything else ? A few of the Highlanders were no doubt conscripts : but there was far less conscription than is commonly the case in war. Although there were Jacobites in England, the fight, quite appropriately, remained in English eyes of the time essentially a Scottish revolt. In Scotland it was never seen as a rift between Highlands and Lowlands : both parts of the country were split by it. If the majority of Scots people did not actively associate themselves with the Jacobites, there were religious and political deterrents : even the staunchest Whigs, like Forbes of Culloden, knew that the Jacobite cause received its support from legitimate and bitter grievances against the Westminster Government. Many were the adherents who came to arms simply out of patriotism, with *No Union* engraved upon the blades of their swords.

The error sedulously propagated by the yes-men of Whiggery that the Union brought immediate prosperity to Scotland is so emphatically falsified by the facts of history that the educated Whig historian describes it rather as a slow process that gathered momentum with the century. I do not think that this either can be substantiated. The industrial age, in whose benefactions and horrors Scotland followed England, came late in the century. The first efforts towards an improved agriculture, in which Scotland led England, were prior to the Union : the work of Fletcher of Saltoun and Cockburn of Ormiston. Likewise with other developments, they were inaugurated prior to 1707, and to a considerable degree atrophied until the middle of the century. The only important development in Edinburgh during her dark age was the founding of the Infirmary, which, however, was itself the offspring of the seventeenth century School of Medicine and originally projected by Sir Andrew Balfour about 1690. The exacerbation of the City is shown by the demonstration against the Government of the Porteous Riot. Then in 1741 and again in 1742 there were grave riots, provoked by the high price of food and the paralysis in the administration. The lack of civic initiative had reduced morale to a level well illustrated by the ludicrous conduct of the levies raised amongst the citizens to defend the Capital, very different from their conduct against Hertford. Jupiter Carlyle of Inveresk was one of them and describes the scorn and derision poured upon them by the ladies at the windows,

who were largely Jacobite in sympathy. Ordered to march out
to meet the Highlanders, the volunteers scuttled almost to a man
into the wynds and doorways of the West Bow, so that when their
leader turned round at the foot of the Bow to exhort them, he
found to his chagrin that he had no troops. Brigadier Fowkes
arrived from London and led the 13th and 14th Dragoons on a
foray towards Coltbridge, where a few Highland gentlemen fired
their pistols at them and promoted the Canter o' Coltbrig, the
dragoons fleeing headlong with what loot they had been able to
gather from the homesteads of Corstorphine, until they got to
Leith, where, a cry being raised in mockery that the Highlanders
were near, they fled again, to Preston Pans (the scene later of
the Prince's spectacular victory), casting their loot and their
weapons as they went. Here one of them fell into a coal-pit, and
his cries inspired his companions to ride without further stop to
North Berwick.

At last all Edinburgh's defenders, the citizens, the men from
Dalkeith and Musselburgh, and the Seceders, had dispersed, leaving
only the rather reluctant garrison in the Castle. Here General
Preston had been superseded in his command for fear lest, as a
Scot, he should prove disloyal, by an Englishman, General Guest.
Guest would have surrendered the Castle but for Preston, who
was in fact one of the dourest old Whigs and bitterly hated the
Stewarts. Preston took over the command again. He had been
seventy years a soldier, was now eighty-six and had to be wheeled
round in a chair to inspect the guard, but he was stern and courageous, only of an ill-nature that made him subject the City and its
unfortunate inhabitants to unjustifiable bombardments. He even
anticipated blitz tactics in sending his soldiers to fire houses in
the High Street and then cannonading the citizens who tried to
put out the flames.

As an illustration of the English attitude to the Scots at that
time, it may be remarked that whereas Guest (who was probably
not a coward but a secret Jacobite sympathiser) received every
honour and award for his services on the occasion, concluding
with a Westminster Abbey burial, old Preston could not even
secure a small pension.

If we except a few men of the calibre of Forbes of Culloden
(whose fine statue by Roubiliac in the Parliament House reflects
a neish integrity), men of true principle and a pragmatic wisdom,
the Scottish Whigs were an ignoble lot at that time. It was
hardly unnatural that their ranks should have been largely
composed of place-seekers and time-servers, and of the merely
embittered : and that most men of spirit and of disinterest should

have been Jacobite in sympathy. There was just grievance with the whole government of the country, and the best of the Whigs showed a considerable sympathy for their opponents after the debacle of Culloden, as well they might.

Prince Charles was everywhere welcomed by the poor people from Edinburgh and round about, whether or not they were prepared to share his desperate adventure. The conduct of the Highlanders in Edinburgh, as elsewhere, was extraordinary. There was not one case of misbehaviour. A few local miscreants actually disguised themselves as Highlanders in the hope of gaining licence, but were quickly rounded up and shot by the Jacobites. Charles's own bearing was modest and dignified. Altogether, it is impossible not to feel, faced by the monstrous deeds of Cumberland's troops, that, while ends cannot justify means, means go a long way to justify ends. The principles of honour and generosity by which the Jacobite army were so singularly distinguished is a better testament to the goodwill of their cause than the mixture of pusillanimity and savagery that stamps their opponents.

Perhaps, after all, although it patently was not the forces of law and order that prevailed, it may have been those of comfort and security. Edinburgh as a whole was relieved by the news of Culloden, but not hysterical or jubilant. The people watched in silence as Cumberland aired his spite by having the banners of Charles and the Chiefs burnt by the common hangman and the sweeps at the Mercat Cross. "A vile spot," and "no place for mild measures," he called our country, and spoke for many in England. Members of the Town Guard, the city's police force, then as now largely Highland, had taken a day off to go to Falkirk to use their Hanoverian muskets in the Prince's cause. The two most eminent Whig lawyers of their own initiative went to Carlisle to defend Jacobites from the shambles : and when eloquence failed, one of them dressed his servant in tartan, so that he was arrested and would have been hanged had his master not proved his alibi with withering scorn upon the conduct of the Law in that town. Fifty years later when a bronze statue of Charles turned up in a cellar of St. Giles, it was placed in the Royal Exchange, discreetly, without a name being put to it. The majority of those grand characters of the later eighteenth century, the strong-flavoured life of Edinburgh so well described by Robert Chambers, remained Jacobite in spirit even when the cause was lost forever. At heart even the Whigs, where they had hearts at all, betray sympathy.

Although the '45 promoted oppressive measures particularly in

61, 62　John Knox's house to-day, and as it was nearly a century ago

63   The Canongate Church

64   Robert Adam's Chapel and chapel-house in York Place
From engravings after T. H. Shepherd (1829)

the Highlands, the Highlands were bound to have suffered, as indeed they already were suffering, from the phases of civilisation for which the Hanoverians stood. I do not think there is any question that the harm, in victimisation, that it brought upon Scotland is comparable to the essential good it did her, a good that was almost immediately made manifest in the Capital. The pipes and the kilts in Edinburgh shook the City out of its forlorn despondency : courage, chivalry, and honour suddenly came to life again, and when the trained English troops were seen to flee, and the London Government to be in panic, the sense of persisting inferiority that the Scots had come to accept, and that their politicians seemed to have justified by their conduct in 1707, lifted like a fousome cloud. The sight of noble men going to the scaffold is disheartening only to the cynical or the obsequious : for others it is a challenge, a call to at least some justification of their manhood. I think that extraordinary, courageous adventure that brought the men from the mountains into the eighteenth century city was the real genesis of the New Town of Edinburgh and of what has been called her Augustan Age. The culture and taste of the townsfolk shaped the squares and streets that spread to the north : but it was the spirit of the people from the far parts of their country that restored to Edinburgh the dignity of a Capital. A Capital without Court or Parliament, but still the true centre of the nation. It is significant that the original project for opening out a New Town, approached by the North Bridge, was the idea of James VII when he was Duke of York and Royal Commissioner at Holyrood. Designs were actually prepared for the bridge by Sir William Bruce. The plan was further developed by the Earl of Mar who, after 1715, during his long exile at Aix-la Chapelle, spent his time drawing designs for the good of the Capital of his beloved country. Even Princes Street was envisaged by him, with gardens running down to the Nor' Loch, which he thought might be cleansed by a canal leading from the Water of Leith. But during those long years of the City's despondency, although the congestion in the Old Town became acute, it seemed that there was no life to do anything. A few days were spent again by a Stewart in Edinburgh supported by the most valiant of his countrymen, and the City took courage.

The only alternative judgments on the result of the '45 are, first, that it harmed Scotland : second, that it was an event of no real or lasting significance to the country. But despite the oppressive measures, often legally unjustifiable, that it called down on Scotland's head, the activity and vitality of her people demonstrably increased to a degree that far offset oppression.

Nor can anyone to-day seriously accept the Victorian judgment on the '45 summed up by Buckle as the " last struggle of barbarism against civilisation " : and with that falls the corollary that the *suppression* of the '45 was the true saving of Scotland, as though a negative (and the Hanoverian revenge was emphatically negative) could have positive fruit. To-day Mr. George Malcolm Thomson's romantic theory is more fashionable. He dismisses it as " a mere episode . . . an anachronism and an anomaly . . . like a dream." The '45 was a fact, it was not a dream. It was the nation's re-surgent spirit that the adventure was able to free, as no sordid prospect of prosperity could ever have freed it. The belittlers can point to concomitant motives, but these no more deny the best than do the many ulterior aspects that confuse every war. Of our recent war, it is not in all its inventive ingenuity that we look for hope for the future : these are aspects that perturb us : it is in the true spirit, held if even only by a minority, that detested the evils against which we fought, and that believed in a glory of life and death.

It was Fletcher of Saltoun who shrewdly observed that " if a man were permitted to write all the ballads he need not care who should make the laws of a nation." It was the Stewarts not the Guelphs who wrote our ballads. The Jacobite Cause inspired all the songs of the aftermath, and gave the impetus to the inter-pretative writing of Scott. It was its heroism that gave the country the reawakening that is not a matter of legislation : and this because it was a true heroism, chivalrous, and singularly little tarnished with hatred or vindictiveness or self-seeking.

v

The Canongate (2) retains considerably more of the traditional Old Town houses than does the High Street, but many of them are now derelict, their future uncertain. It seems to bypass the intelligence of so many of our countrymen that a City has no immortal soul : they are gey proud of an ancient burgh, but will not hesitate to demolish all the buildings that are evidence of its antiquity and needful to the sustenance of its tradition. There are ancient burghs in Scotland that do not retain a single house of a respectable antiquity : they have renounced their birthright and are merest shanty towns in which pride of age is ludicrous. These old houses are all that the majority ever ken of history : they are history, and many of them are or have been beautiful.

To remove them all and replace them with whatever biggins are the fashion of the uneasy day would not be to renew Edinburgh, but to construct a new and dubious city upon the site of an old, historic and honourable one.

Near the head of the Canongate are a number of blocks of good houses ; simple or more elaborate, all are expressions of the City's past and essential character. The now deserted Morocco Land has a grotesque carved figure of a Moor and a pleasant legend attached to it. Lower down is the last of the double-decker houses, with two rows of dormers in its roof line, a fine frontage. Several houses retain stair towers, round or octagonal. There are closes behind. Chessels Court is a late development of the tradition : it has some florid plasterwork within, and forms with Pirrie's Close an open court that could be made delightful. Playhouse Close is the site of the Canongate Theatre, opened two years after the '45, the first regular theatre to survive puritan zeal in the City. It was run by a good English company : the stars being Lee and Digges, Mrs. Bellamy and Mrs. Ward. It had various managers, including David Beatt who had read Prince Charles's proclamation at the Mercat Cross. But the Canongate Theatre can only claim a modest, local renown : it is no monument to the art of the stage, like the Globe or the Abbey or the Comedie, even although the one Scottish play of the century was first produced there.

Scotland's lack of a drama since the Reformation has already been commented upon. The puritanical hegemony, even long since it finally failed to banish the theatre altogether, has a continued disservice to its credit, for the drama has yet to become a mode of national expression. *Douglas*, the Rev. John Home's tragedy, although it outraged the Kirk and finished his ministerial career, received a tremendous reception. An enthusiastic rather than discriminating member of its first audience is reported to have cried " Whaur's your Wullie Shakespeare noo ! " expressing the excitement of an audience that had had to depend entirely upon an imported drama when presented with anything even remotely appertaining to Scotland. It is of course poor, thin stuff : the merest localising of the wersh tragedies of the eighteenth century, in stilted English blank verse, drawing nothing, unlike the poetry of Fergusson, from the living Scotland. Yet even such discriminating persons as David Hume were delighted with it, and John Home became a popular hero. A similar state of affairs is revealed many years later when, the Canongate being no longer a fashionable quarter, its theatre had been killed by the old Theatre Royal (79) at the New Town end of the North Bridge, on the site of the present G.P.O. This theatre which had flourished for a time with the Kembles, the Siddonses, the Boy Roscius, and other lights chiefly of the London stage, had reached a financial crisis when Scott came forward with the operatic dramatisation of *Rob Roy*. This had already had some success at Covent Garden. It opened in Edinburgh on 15th February 1819, and was received with a wild enthusiasm that changed the whole fortunes of the theatre. A series of Waverley dramas followed, although *Rob Roy* outlived the lave. I saw it myself as a boy in Edinburgh almost exactly a hundred years later, still played in the old barn-storming manner amongst hisses and cheers. It was good hearty stuff, essentially stagey, written for an existing dramatic fashion, but was never more. It had never, like the Shakespearean stage been the expression of a people, writing and acting fused to those heights of interpretation where the particular blossoms into universality. Although Edinburgh maintained throughout the last century, with Dublin, the most creditable depot of the London stage, and Irving amongst other famous actors started his career here before an audience always regarded as testing, it was never anything more. In Scotland we have yet to experience the spontaneous combustion that produced a native Irish theatre in Dublin forty years ago : and at the moment Glasgow, with its Citizen's Theatre, may be first in the field, if that venture outgrows its initial tendency to be cosmopolitan from the wrong end—I refer, of course, to that applied cosmopolitan " culture," always a substitute article so long as there is no native stock on to which it may be grafted. At present native Scottish drama is practically confined to the traditional comics ; to couthy pieces written to any slightly dated London pattern ; and to Mr. Bridie, whose *Forrigan Reel*, in its first, Glasgow version, gave us hopes that he might return from working Barrie's pitch on the export trade.

VI

The Canongate Tolbooth (2) has outlived Edinburgh's ancient seat of civic government and town gaol. Dated 1592, it is a good example of its kind, with its tower and corbelled turrets, forestair and high dormer-heads. Some day, perhaps, the outsize Victorian clock will be replaced.

The Tolbooth stands, an emphatic expression of history, amongst a number of other fine buildings. Huntly House, opposite, pushes out its two upper floors behind a plastered wood facing. It is dated 1570, and has been renovated as a City Museum.

65, 66   The Greyfriars' Churchyard.   *From photographs taken about 1845 by D. O. Hill*

67 Moray House

68 West Bow from the Lawnmarket

From engravings after Thomas H. Shepherd (1829)

An agreeable wide pend leads through it into Bakehouse Close (57), from which the courtyard of Acheson House is entered. This interesting mansion of a one-time Joint Secretary of State has also fortunately been restored. Over the door it bears the date 1633 and the Acheson crest, a cock standing on a trumpet. In Mr. MacLevy's day " The Cock and Trumpet " was notorious. Between these two mansions is a small house, now a pub with the upper floors deserted, which well merits restoration for the sake of a particularly good group. A little up the street stands Moray House (67), with its striking pyramidal gateway and the balcony, boldly corbelled, from which the Argyle wedding party looked down upon Montrose as he was drawn in ignominous procession from the Water Yett at the foot of the Canongate to his execution at the Edinburgh Cross. Later, Argyle, his bride-groom son, and some of the wedding guests, followed the same passage to the cross. Moray House is now a training college for teachers : its gardens, which were once a popular promenade, are bleakly cemented, and save for three splendid ceilings all the rich interior has gone. Opposite is Shoemakers' Land, built by the Guild in 1677 : also known as Bible Land on account of the open Bible carved below the insignia of a paring knife, crowned, supported by two pawky cherubs.

Golfer's Land is another old friend amongst this company. The story commemorated on the house in the Latin lines of Dr. Pitcairn records that it was built by John Patersone, a shoemaker, with the money won in a wager by him and the Duke of York, playing at the golf against two English noblemen. It is supposed that Patersone was not always so successful, for he died bankrupt. Queensberry House is large, but gaunt and grim, having been converted into a barracks in 1810, it being now a poor's house. It was the scene of a grisly incident on the day of the signing of the Act of Union. The second Duke of Queensberry, Lord High Commissioner, chief and most highly paid promoter of the Act in Scotland, had an idiot son of gorilla-like physique (Grant observes that his vast stature may still be judged from the plain leaden coffin in the family vault at Durisdeer). He was kept in a room with boarded windows at the stairfoot of the west wing, but his keeper having gone out with the rest of the household to watch the tumult in the streets, the monster broke open the door and smelt his way to the kitchen, where a solitary turnspit was turning a roast. When the ducal party returned they found the monstrous heir tearing the roast with his teeth while the little kitchen boy hung impaled and cooking on his own spit. It was cried " a judgment."

The poet Gay stayed for some time with the third Duke, and frequented a celebrated public, Jenny Ha's Change House, which stood next to Golfer's Land. But madness persisted in the Queensberry family, whose main line died out, and the Earl of March, who inherited, was that remarkable character of the London of George III : " Old Q," a debauchee who at an advanced age entertained a company in his drawing-room by acting, *touts nus*, Paris judging the goddesses and presenting his apple. In spite of such absurdities, he was renowned and frequently consulted for his profound political wisdom. It was " Old Q " who had Queensberry House stripped and sold up.

On the north side again, the White Horse Close (59) is an attractive piece of the past. The east and west sides have been altered, but the north side is much as it was, with its forestairs leading into overhanging timbered gables. It was formerly an inn, but it is not that White Horse Inn at which Johnson and Boswell met, and which stood at the head of the Canongate in St. Mary's Wynd—one of those perjinked to the status of a street and filled with the dour, relentless, extremely well-built, Scotostyle tenements that followed the Improvement Act of 1867. Before then it had become one of the filthiest in Edinburgh. These inns of Edinburgh were, as Johnson discovered, slovenly places, their chief importance being as change-houses : the White Horse had stabling for upwards of a hundred horses. It was customary for those who intended to make a long stay to go to a lodging-house, of which there were many advertising select accommodation.

The Canongate Church (63) stands back from the Tolbooth, and from the surviving cross. It was built in 1688 for the congregation ousted from the Abbey Church by James VII. The exterior is agreeable, with its suggestion of baroque, its pillared portico, and the finial of (genuine) stag's horns supporting a cross, insignia of the burgh. Inside it is at present cumbered with one of those vast organs that have commonly been allowed to dominate Kirk interiors since kists of whistles were allowed within the precincts. The Scots assuredly are extremists—one way or another !

St. John Street is interesting as a forerunner of the New Town. It is entered in the old way, through a particularly wide pend, but the street is broad and its houses have areas and are distinctively eighteenth century in character. They are quite small, although they were originally the homes of wealthy and distinguished persons ; aristocrats, judges, and country gentlemen. In their day they must have seemed most desirable bijoux residences, with a privacy denied in the old lands. They were building in 1768, but the house with the pend is a little earlier. It was the home of Tobias Smollett's sister, and from here he gathered his Edinburgh material for *Humphrey Clinker*. It has a round stair tower to the back.

St. John Street leads to the South Back of the Canongate, now known as Holyrood Road, which joins up with the Cowgate. The Cowgate retains practically nothing ancient or interesting, except its own curious tunnelling quality, boring its way through below the heights, under South Bridge and George IV Bridge, to open out into the Grassmarket. The buildings to the front of Tailors' Hall were recently demolished, but not long since hoisted a fine flourish of lum and gablet. During the dark age it was the favourite haunt of such strolling players from England as succeeded in storming the barns of Edinburgh. Now only the Magdalene Chapel remains of the Cowgate's glories. The chapel, with almshouses, was endowed and built in 1541 for the Hammermens' Guild. It is notable in having the only mediæval stained glass to survive in Scotland : four roundels of coats of arms. It is a clinic now, but the chapel is still attractive, with the painted arms of guilds. It is possible that beneath the present plaster ceiling, and no doubt overpainted, there may be mediæval paintings on the wooden barrel-vault. There is a neat little steeple of 1622. This chapel and the hulk of Trinity College are the only two survivors of the many mediæval chapels in the burgh.

Except for the White Hart Inn there is little of interest left in the Grassmarket, and yet somehow it is a cheerful and engaging place, so wide, with the Castle rising dramatically above it. But the foot of the West Bow has the best unbroken array of Old Town façades, now on their last legs but pre-eminently worthy of preservation. Their varied gables—plain, crow-stepped, ogival—facing the street, with doocots above the attics, make a brave show from the upper level, and are most expressive of the seventeenth century aspect of the City's character. The West Bow (68), although the line has been straightened into Victoria Street, remains singularly charming, with its double level of buildings and the curving slope with which it pours itself into the open Grassmarket below. It has shops of a good kind : ironmongers, dairy-utensilmen, cord-and-moleskin tailors, and brush-makers' shops with old signs, selling hornware and wooden cuppies, the usual plenishing of working-class homes of not so very long ago. These are shops tended by the aristocracy of tradesfolk, like the old lady who until lately kept a toyshop in the Grassmarket, with toys that had been in her stock for fifty years. I bought jumping-jacks and Dutch dolls from her, marked down because the worm had got into their legs. And I mind of a black-out night, walking along the upper pavement behind two of our most remarkable present-day personalities, scholarly patriots, one more than a foot taller than the other, when a girl's voice came up sweetly, clearly from the Bow below, singing not in those frantic noises that scream the death of a civilisation, but an unforgettable Jacobite song.

Hamilton's measured drawings of both sides of the Bow before it was altered show the most fantastic and enchanting variety of houses. They included Major Weir's, left empty for more than a hundred years, and long the terror of children and of night passengers down the Bow. Major Weir, like Deacon Brodie, is a character of a kind that always seems peculiarly to endear itself to the Scots imagination. It was he who led Montrose to the scaffold, and who habitually led in prayer the unco-guids who particularly congregated in the Bow. None could approach him for fervour, zeal, and cant. And then he suddenly confessed, without contrition, to a life of the most sordid crime, spiced with witchcraft, for which he was burnt at the stake.

Candlemaker Row, the southern slope up from the Grassmarket, has some old houses, notably Candlemaker Hall, with its two square towers, restored by the City and now put to excellent purpose as the Edinburgh Press Club. Its small, panelled hall is delightful, and looks out over the Greyfriars kirkyard (69), where the Franciscan monastery stood until it was utterly despoiled by Argyle and his Reformers in 1559. The Greyfriars kirk (70) which later replaced it is renowned for the signing there of the National Covenant. It was one of the Edinburgh churches most damaged by Oliver Cromwell. It is rather a sad-looking edifice, but its graveyard has a splendid array of tombs (65, 66), from which unfortunately and most mistakenly, the ironwork was removed during the late war.

69   The Churchyard

70   The Church

GREYFRIARS

71   The University : the Old Quad

New Town and Augustan Age

The Setting—August Personalities—Building of the New Town—
Public Buildings—The Disruption

I

THE END OF THE EIGHTEENTH CENTURY AND THE BEGINNING of the nineteenth saw the birth and growth of the New Town of Edinburgh. It is the outstanding phase of the City's history since the Reformation. In the classical parlance of the day it was her Augustan Age, and she the Modern Athens. Self-conscious no doubt, but self-confident forbye, these years saw her wear a flaunted coif of culture, develop her older traditions into a solid certitude and her ancient houses into stews of destitution and depravity. Crime increased vastly in the City after 1770 as the wynds became more and more the homes of the unfortunates of the Industrial Age. Palliatives were slow in coming. Even half a century later, Dr. Guthrie had fierce opposition to his schemes. Part of the trouble was religious. The industrial schools were supported by the new tradition of enlightened, Radical, Whigs, who took the view that in order to secure the attendance of many poor children of Irish origin, the schools should be interdemoninational, with religious instruction by the various clergy. Although the omnipotence of the Kirk had disappeared with surprising rapidity, bitter bigotry persisted. The Kirk that up till 1747 had prevented the foundation of a theatre, was, before the turn of the century adapting the times of the meetings of its General Assembly so that they would not be depleted by the rival attraction of Mrs. Siddons at the Theatre Royal. And within itself it was heading for its historic split of 1843.

Before the Irish invasion there was a considerable influx of Highlanders fleeing before the politically abetted evictions to which Dr. Johnson applied " they make a wilderness and they call it peace." By the 1780s there was a Gaelic Chapel in the Grassmarket for those who had no English whatever. It seated eleven hundred, and there were requests for three hundred seats over and above that number. Many of the Highlanders, moreover, were Catholics or Episcopalians, and the former had their own Gaelic chapel in the Blackfriars Wynd.

From all parts of the Lowlands, too, people gravitated into Edinburgh. On the whole they did better than those who went to such mushroom communities as Glasgow. For the expansion was not so rapid as to constitute essentially a new community, rootless and inchoate. Edinburgh had her past, which for all its motley and change set upon her that palpable if largely indefinable sense of form that we loosely call tradition. She had that often obnoxious and ridiculous, but to any civilised urban community essential commodity (however much those who have doubts in man's intrinsic equality may deplore it), a definable caste system. Despite the gradual atrophy of our aristocracy, impoverished and with a declining responsibility—part culpable, part inevitable with the decline in land values : it for long served Edinburgh well by heading the hierarchy, with leisure and means to encourage the arts, and with, on its own behalf, grand qualities of character and intransigeance. Gradually, however, most of the noble families changed their winter residence from Edinburgh to London. By that Edinburgh was the loser, Scotland suffered a vast increment of absentee landlordism, and the Scottish aristocracy largely lost its identity and any reason for its existence. However, immediately below the noble families there was that large body of the lairdry : remarkable for its independence, intelligence, and consistence. Often extremely poor, they were ever more impressed by pedigree than by material wealth, which seems always to have shocked and puzzled the English. Burt, an officer of engineers under Wade, was disgusted by such incidents as the sight of a laird leaping from his horse to embrace an innkeeper, who, he explained, was of good family, but a younger son and had had to take to trade. It was in fact no mean assessment of quality : and to this day it is notable that Scots of all walks of life know the names and associations of their great-grandparents, a matter in which the English are customarily quite ignorant. It is in its best a civilised respect for tradition and forbears, rather in the Chinese manner, giving a stabilising sense of continuity and responsibility. It may decline in the present social anarchy, but it is probably quite vigorous enough to revive, and to survive the era of civil-service and intellectual snobbery that tends to replace it to-day. It is strange how much more reassuring it is to hear a black-coated clerk say with pride and pleasure, " My grandfather was a farmer in the Mearns," than to hear him tell with inevitable smugness, " My father was in the Customs, and I am in the Ministry of Transport."

72 Looking down Princes Street from Calton Hill. *From a print by J. Gendall* (1824)

73 Lt.-Col. Batty's view of the Royal High School (*c.* 1830)

74   Houses in George Square

75   Detail of entry to 48 Queen
Street

76   Ironwork in North Charlotte
Street

The lairds constantly stocked the professions, keeping their roots in the country, enjoying their sport, and often ably assisting the improvement of agriculture. Glasgow may sneer at them : but those who made their money out of Glasgow real estate were quick to carry it elsewhere, and left that city to a hierarchy of trade that had few graces, and its corporation to become a tragic byword for corruption. Glasgow, an ancient and once most beautiful city, suffered from such a violent expansion as leaves her to this day in a most unfortunate state of formlessness. Edinburgh has so far been able to absorb her incomers : although to-day she faces a renewed threat to her integrity.

The twenty years between 1790 and 1810 seem to have been the peak period of Augustan Edinburgh. The Napoleonic wars brought many visitors from England and beyond who found the city elegant and refined, and interesting in its distinctive character. Sir Walter Scott brought a tremendous stimulus, making his countrymen house-proud as it were ; giving their history and environment that gloss that is one of the greatest values of a country's literature, supplying an imaginative interpretation of its life that enriches the consciousness of its people. No doubt his romanticism lay a little heavy, no doubt by the highest canons he lacked the plummet-like dive of universality, the ultimate integrity : he was a giant for all that. There are points at which Tobias Smollett, John Galt, and Susan Ferrier have each a greater aesthetic integrity than Scott, and a surer touch : none of them occupy a like place in the history of their country. Stevenson had a greater scunner than Scott, and a keener apprehension. He suffered, and Scotland suffered, by his having to emigrate from Edinburgh to the distant island from whence he wrote in restlessness : " It is a singular thing that I should live here in the South Seas and yet my imagination so continually inhabits the cold old huddle of grey hills from which we came." His house in Inverleith Row is a fusty little museum displaying the ends of the bed on which he was born and many faded photographs ; and Scott's incredible monument houses, without piety or meaning, assorted alto-relievo effigies of Mary and Knox, George Buchanan and Charles I. But these are no testament to their merits, unless the sheer size of the Scott Monument carries a suggestion of the vastness of Scott's activities in his native city. His life in Edinburgh is impressive in the width of its associations : his gargantuan appetite for employing himself in literature, antiquities, politics, the theatre, the volunteers, the entertaining of decadent royalty. He was often ludicrous and occasionally unjust in a way in which the balanced Cockburn, his friend and political opponent, could never have been. But he had an enthusiasm that even Cockburn could not muster. And his love of his country was warm and instant, not deflected, as Cockburn's could have been, by the surreptitious sentimentality of the over-reaching brotherhood of man evinced in public meetings.

II

With less imagination, Cockburn was shrewder than Scott, and the *Memorials of His Own Time* give a remarkable picture of the Augustan Age, its aftermath, and, by implication and reference, of the age that immediately preceded it. He was, unlike Scott, of the progressive faction, but in this an excellent judgment tempered his enthusiasm. He writes with real respect and affection of the older generation of Judges, understanding that they were simply incapable of appreciating the changes that were taking place. As a reformer he never weakened after failure, and was remarkably unaffected by that reforming vanity whereby the brave new world is seen as an absolute renaissance instead of merely the reassertion of values that have been submerged by the efforts of his predecessors. Therefore he avoided the modern folly of discarding tradition without consideration whether the very bases of reform will not be jettisoned with it. He avoided, too, the puritannical urge to force others to his way of thinking and behaving. He was a leader amongst those persons of judgment who were actively concerned to preserve Edinburgh from the worst follies of ignorant Councillors and jobbing speculators during its initial periods of expansion. Often their efforts failed, but they persisted and gradually they were more successful : and it is largely to Cockburn that we owe the preservation of Princes Street as a boulevard and of an uncluttered Mound.

Cockburn was one of the Counsel for the Defence in the Burke and Hare trials, in 1828, undeterred by the public hysteria— highly understandable as it was, since the anatomy murders implied that anyone was worth murdering for his carcase alone. He was able to observe of Burke : " Except that he murdered, Burke was a sensible, and what might be called a respectable man ; not at all ferocious in his general manner, sober, correct in all his other habits, and kind to his relations."

Cockburn began his long life in 1779, and as a young man met, and pled before, the ancient school of Scottish Judges, of whom he leaves some delightful accounts. There was Lord Monboddo, who believed that men had once had tails, and indeed suspected all midwives of being in a plot to remove the rudimentary appendage from every new-born baby. He was a man of great classical learning and excellent conversation, if rather given to paradox : and even Dr. Johnson had to drop his bias against him on his memorable visit with Boswell. His gracious qualities were conjoined with oddities of that emphatic and natural kind that remains one of the chief delights of the Scottish character. As a Judge he once pled his own case in litigation against a man in whose care his horse had died. To his extreme disgust he lost it. Ever after he refused to sit at the Bench, but took his place at the Clerk's table. This he found agreeable, since it enabled him to slip easily out of Court during any pause or delay and have a crack with friends in the Outer House. Even when old, he frequently rode to London on horseback, where he shone in literary society. His villa in St. John Street was renowned for its excellent talk and table. It was kept by his daughter, whom all authorities, from Robert Burns to the dowagers of the day, credit as being the most beautiful of all the City's beauties. She refused marriage to remain with her father, but died of consumption in her early twenties to his great distress.

Very different was Lord Braxfield. He was the intellectual giant of the Law, fierce and relentless, arguing colloquially with question and answer in broad Scots—and yet with a contempt for letters and all refinement. Many of his most remarkable sayings have had to perish, being unprintable. Those that have survived display an amazing invincible scunner, which Cockburn puts down not to cruelty, " for which he was too strong and too jovial, but from cherished coarseness." He was savagely vindictive in the political trials during the Jacobin scare. When the unfortunate Gerald said that all great men had been reformers, " even our Saviour himself," Braxfield muttered, " Muckle he made o' that. He was hangit ! " Braxfield's successor as head of the Criminal Court was Lord Eskgrove, also gifted, but ridiculous in his portentousness. In condemning to death some robbers who had broken into the house of Luss and assaulted the inmates on a Sunday, he came by slow stages to his climax : " . . . All this you did ; and God preserve us ! joost when they were sitten doon to their denner ! " Lord Kames is responsible for the most mordant chess story, when he sentenced to death a murderer with whom he had often played, with the postscript, " That's checkmate noo, Matthie ! "

Cockburn leaves a most affectionate portrait of Lord Hermand, an active and joyous judge, who hated repose, except in bed where

" he slept zealously. . . . Was he in argument, or at whist, or over his wine ; in Court, or at an election, or a road-meeting ; consulting with a ploughman or talking with a child ; he was sure to blaze out in a style that nobody could have fancied, or could resist enjoying." He had " a conversational wildness, made more delightful by the undoubted sincerity of the passing extravagance. . . . Had he depended on his understanding alone, or chiefly, he would have been wrecked every week. But honesty, humanity, social habits, and diverting public explosions, always kept him popular ; and he lived about eighty-four years, with keen and undisguised feelings and opinions, without ever being alienated from a friend, or imagining a shabby action, devoted to rural occupations, keeping up his reading, and maintaining his interest in the world by cultivating the young . . . and he had acted in more of the severest scenes of old Scotch drinking than any man at last living. Commonplace topers think drinking a pleasure ; but with Hermand it was a virtue." It was Hermand who with the greatest sincerity called for sentence on a man who had killed a friend in a drunken wrangle, exploding, " Good God, my Laards, if he will do this when he's drunk, what will he not do when he's sober ? "

Lord Newton, who drowsily expectant stares at us from the Raeburn portrait in the Scottish National Gallery, was another of the great drinking judges. There is a story of a Frenchman arriving in the City, carousing all night with a chance acquaintance, and, with a bad hangover, making the sightseer's visit to the Courts in the morning, where he was surprised to recognise in the imposing Lord Newton his companion of the night before, now calmly and composedly administering justice. He had a phenomenal ability of dozing during dull and irrelevant pleading, to awaken sharply when Counsel came to any important point.

III

Edinburgh's eighteenth century wing lies to the north of the Old Town, but there was an earlier annexe to the south built by a speculative builder, James Brown, in 1766. Of this George Square (74) remains, particularly pleasant, its more formal houses varied with some of red and blue stone to a chequered pattern, in a rustic fashion that aggravated Edinburgh's historian of the time, Hugo Arnot, who compared them to " sailors' shirts." Lord Braxfield moved into the Square ; Scott spent much of his youth

77 Head office of the Royal Bank of Scotland, St. Andrew's Square, originally built as a town house by Sir William Chambers

78 Sir Walter Scott's house in Castle Street

79   The old Theatre Royal in Shakespeare Square

80   The New Assembly Rooms in George Street

From engravings after T. H. Shepherd (1829)

in number 25 ; and Jamieson, who compiled the first dictionary of Scots was another of many notable residents of its earlier days. Buccleuch Street that flanks it to the south was built in 1780, after the magistrates, who had refused to undertake the southern development, were already proceeding with the New Town. South again lie the Meadows, originally the Burgh Loch which had been drained earlier in the eighteenth century, contiguous with Bruntsfield Links, part of the old Burgh Muir. These were left to form an open space when a hundred years later the City next expanded in this airt with streets of superior, and well-built, Victorian terraces and villas.

The land to the north of the Nor' Loch, the chosen site for the New Town, was singularly bare of houses. Only one house within its compass to-day dates from a much earlier period, this is the little mansion of Easter Coates (60), built in 1600, since added to, and quite dwarfed by Gilbert Scott's vast Episcopalian Cathedral to which it now serves as deanery. Provost Drummond was the active promoter of the scheme, and James Craig the author of the successful plan for its lay out. Princes Street was so called after George IV and his brother : it was to have been called St. Giles Street, but George III protested on account of the association with the poor ward of London. At first people were reluctant to move so far furth of the Old Town. The Corporation had to offer a bribe of £20 for the first person to build himself a house in the area : the house still stands, rather independent of the main plan, in Thistle Court. An exemption of all burghal taxes was granted a silk mercer for inaugurating Princes Street with a mansion next to the Register House that, long overdue, had been built for the country's records to the design of Robert Adam.

Craig's plan was practically unaltered during the building, which went on through the last thirty years of the eighteenth century, until the whole of the original New Town was completed. The simple forthright layout is excellent, and the site, which is admirably used, prevents it from being dull. The boulevard of Princes Street (20) commands a dramatic view of the Castle, from it the transverse streets rise to George Street on the crest of the ridge, and descend again to where Queen Street, above its gardens, forms a break on the northern slope. George Street was originally conceived as the main street : its houses were considerably grander than those of Princes Street, and it terminates in two fine squares. The architecture was respectable, if not for the most part distinguished. Only the north side of Charlotte Square (88) achieves real magnificence. Imposing yet delicate, Adam's façade is as good a thing of its kind as can be seen anywhere. Unfortunately he died before the rest of the Square was completed, and it bears the heavy overstamp of Sir Robert Reid, architect of the Parliament House frontage. Despite much protest, Adam's original design for St. George's Church was jettisoned for the less expensive and inferior work of Playfair (91) (all the same, seen down the vista of George Street, that green dome is a great pleasure : and the portico is dignified enow). At the east end Adam built the two blocks flanking the present Royal Bank (77) in St. Andrew Square, the Bank being itself the work of another Scottish architect with many English buildings to his credit, Sir William Chambers. In Queen Street number 8 is an Adam house, built for Baron Orme, whose daughter is reputed to have chalked the name St. David Street on the neighbouring cross-road, and so canonised David Hume who had newly moved there from the heights above. It is now treated with little respect by the Post Office. The Queen Street houses are of considerable variety : some of them pretty good (75), but mostly marred by petty additions. In Castle Street there are some round-bowed houses with rusticated basements including Scott's (78), sometimes reputed by Adam. The Assembly Rooms (80) of 1787 and a few other buildings remain to us of the good George Street houses. But often the merit of the individual houses is largely sustained by the fine stone from Craigleith Quarry, once a silvery grey, and the excellent craftsmanship of their construction.

The second New Town development was begun in 1809, in a little pocket on the Leith side of Broughton Street. The Forth Street houses here retain marks of considerable merit. The complete plan was never finished, but in 1815 it was being continued below Queen Street Gardens, west from Drummond Place, by Abercromby Place and Heriot Row, Great King Street, Northumberland Street, as far as Royal Circus, and north to the near side of Fettes Row, beyond which order gives place pretty abruptly to the chaos that was consummated in the Great Railway Age when the lines gashed their way through the growing City. The demand for houses was insistent now, and the whole area was built up in a very few years. Although there is here nothing so good as the Adam work (indeed, by this time Adam's work, was considered frippery and the taste was for something more austere, as of Athens rather than Spoleto), Playfair and Hamilton were two creditable architects. Hamilton's individual buildings are the better, but Playfair had a flair both for the bold lay-out and for niceties of interior decoration. An interesting recapitulation of the Edinburgh lands is reflected in India Street, amongst others, where although the façades give an appearance of separate

81   The New Observatory and Playfair's Monument, Calton Hill

82   Robert Adam's Register House
From engravings after T. H. Shepherd (1829)

83 Gillespie Graham's Grecian façade in Moray Place

street houses, the internal arrangements are those of flats—one door entering perhaps one unit, and the next two or three extending over the joint fronts. It is a harmless deceit, and an excellent means of retaining unity while providing houses of varying accommodation.

About the same time private enterprise began the third element of the New Town, across Queensferry Street with Melville Street. The building here is less stern again, with nice ironwork. The fourth unit joined the third with the second by the development of the Earl of Moray's property between the two. An opportunity was missed here by making the houses of Moray Place (83), Ainslie Place (86) and Randolph Crescent (87) face away from the high cliff above the Water of Leith which would have provided a splendid foreground for a more formal elevation. Even now the height of wall above the wooded depths has grandeur : and the view from the windows, over the tree-tops to the Forth, is a glorious one. Gillespie Graham was the architect, and his work, while dignified, as in the pillared fronts of Moray Place, is always somewhat heavy.

The crowning achievement of the orderly planning of the New Town was unfortunately never completed for lack of funds. This was Playfair's lay out of 1819 for the north-eastern link-up of Edinburgh with Leith. Its beginnings lay in the building on the terraces constructed by Stevenson's engineer grandfather on the lower slope of the Calton Hill, of Carlton Terrace, Regent Terrace, and Royal Terrace. The last is an astonishing austere façade nearly a quarter of a mile long, impressively monotonous but proffering a spectacular background for the streets that were to have been built below it to the north, of which Leopold Place is one of the only ones that was actually completed. Royal Terrace became the home of merchants who could watch for their ships coming into Leith from its windows, and was nicknamed Whisky Row. In the angle of the Calton behind it the gardens are beautifully laid out by Sir James Paxton of Crystal Palace fame. A strange freak is provided by the houses of Blenheim Place, its western approach. Apparently these are only basemented bungalows but they flaunt massive chimney stacks to serve the three-storey houses beneath them entered from the lower level of Greenside, whose burn is now a scavenger confined to a conduit.

The New Town phase of building actually continued almost to the close of the nineteenth century. But its quality declined steadily, until fine masonry can hardly lend dignity to elevations indifferent or downright bad. Bow windows protrude with coarse emphasis : roof parapets become graceless. There is the beginning of a very late row on the Queensferry Road where the stone has been tortured to simulate stucco. But even in the worst of them the rooms are often finely proportioned, and the quality of the joinery and plastering is remarkable, far better than that prevailing in London at the same time. Only it has lost in refinement, just as the elevations have lost their sweeping confidence, and we realise afresh that however far Playfair, Hamilton, and Gillespie Graham fall below the Adam standard, they are architects of an exceptional achievement.

Here and there are pockets and off-shoots of the earlier tradition. There must at one time have been an effort to make a respectable residential area in the Morrison Street neighbourhood, near its junction with Lothian Road. Gardner's Crescent (89) here has horizontal astragals gaily carrying on the joints of the masonry along a curving pilastered façade. Across the way Ladyfield Place contains only two exquisite little houses, and then has been forever suspended by the irruption of the railway lines. Around Comely Bank some pleasant little streets run in odd directions, mostly fairly late. Along Leith Walk, Gayfield Place is a notable block, an eighteenth century land with a hint of the Old Town about its curves and unpredictable plan. Gayfield Square alongside was part of the 1809 development and a fashionable place when it was built on the policies of the charming little eighteenth century mansion of Gayfield (85), which remains with its pediment and curly gables.

Sir Henry Raeburn, who was born in a cottage at Stockbridge by the Water of Leith, the son of a yarn worker in one of the mills there, bought ground in his native neighbourhood and built Ann Street, a most delightful and intimate street, its houses fronted by gardens, also Danube Street and, at the instigation of his fellow artist, Sir David Wilkie, the rather portentous, heavily pillared, but amusing St. Bernard's Crescent. On the other side of Edinburgh at Newington, pleasantly situated on the southern slope, there are a number of houses of the earlier nineteenth century, including some Grecian bungalows with massive pillars.

IV

Robert Adam had an ambition to design public buildings on a considerable scale. In this Edinburgh afforded him his best opportunities with the Register House (82) and the University (71)

84 The Sir William Bruce house of Prestonfield

85 The eighteenth-century mansion of Gayfield

86   Houses in Ainslie Place

87   Randolph Crescent : most of the top stories have been altered

88   Charlotte Square: the north side

89   Gardner's Crescent

90   The Castle from the West End, above St. John's and St. Cuthbert's
churches

91   St. George's, Charlotte Square

(although here again he never completed his effect with the steeple (43), which was added much later). The University is a *tour de force* with its triumphant overcoming of the difficulty presented by a steep slope : and its library hall is a magnificent room. The University, or strictly speaking College of Edinburgh as it still was, had gained considerably in reputation at the time, with Dugald Stewart the leader of a distinguished senatus. It is the youngest of Scotland's four universities, having been endowed just before the Reformation by Bishop Reid, although not founded until the reign of James VI, and then constituted under the City authorities. Medicine of course remains its most notable faculty. Until the erection of Adam's Old Quad (71), it had always been rather miserably housed.

At the end of Princes Street with the inauguration of the New Town there had sprung up a huddle of mean houses, surrounding Shakespeare Square (now no more) and the rather tawdry Theatre Royal. These were only swept away, as Cockburn ironically observes, because of the need for an approach to the new prison beneath the Calton Hill. There were two prisons. The first, the Bridewell or House of Correction, was an Adam castellated work (72), similar in character to his Old Observatory which still stands high on the Hill. The main gaol was a silly confection by Elliot and looked something like a toy fort. Cockburn deplored the putting of so splendid a site to such use. The prisons were recently cleared away. The penal cells have been replaced by cellular office accommodation behind a pompous exterior *à la mode,* and the civil servants of St. Andrews House toil where the tread-mill turned before. This fine site has yet to be fittingly graced.

The new High School (73) just beyond has also a grand site, looking out over Holyrood, the Canongate, and the pleasant pagodas of distilleries, to Arthur's Seat. By Thomas Hamilton, it is a really masterly Athenian achievement, a copy of the Temple of Theseus, imposingly set on the curve of the hill. The ironwork before the podium that formerly gave delightful contrast with the massive masonry was foolishly allowed to be removed. The ancient, tough old High School, that once educated peers and peasants at the same desks, and has produced many celebrities, was housed here in 1829. It is now to remove again, to some out-of-the-way suburb. One hopes that the building will not be demolished. It would serve excellently for the National Portrait Gallery collection at present so meanly housed along with the Antiquarian's Museum in Queen Street, and it is surely the out-standing achievement of the Edinburgh Athenian conceit. Play-fair's Royal Scottish Academy and National Gallery (6) at the

Mound, although pleasant, cannot compare with Hamilton's High School.

On the Calton Hill itself stands the unfinished Parthenon, memorial to the Scots killed in the Napoleonic wars. " Scotland's Pride and Poverty " it was called, because funds were inadequate for its completion. As such it is a tribute to poverty : for it looks far better as a traceried ruin on the Calton skyline than it would have looked solid and complete, top-heavy for the Hill. Playfair was the architect, and he also built the new observatory (81), the monument to Playfair, his astronomer uncle, and the scholarly Lysicratean monument to Dugald Stewart : all on the Calton Hill. Opposite the High School is Hamilton's rather inappropriate copy of the Lysicrates monument in honour of Burns. In the neighbouring Calton graveyard by far the finest monument is the Roman piece done for David Hume by Robert Adam. Of the Calton Hill's living residents the most notable was David Octavius Hill, one of the first, and perhaps the greatest of all photographers (11, 65, 66, 92, 93). He had his studio at Rock House, most attractively situated and having splendid views across the City.

There is only one blight on the Calton Hill, and that is the ridiculous Nelson monument, which looks as though it were constructed of outsize cotton reels. It is all too visible, and drops a time-ball down its mast when the one o'clock gun goes off at the Castle.

The Gothic Revival impinged upon the New Town before 1800 with one ecclesiastical building of the Otranto School. This was St. George's Episcopal Chapel built by Robert Adam in York Place. Its adjacent rectory is a masterly piece of fun, battlemented, machicolated and balustered, but all so discreetly that it hardly breaks the line of the street. Unfortunately the Chapel, which was Scott's place of worship after his conversion to the Episcopal persuasion, was lately converted into a showroom for bathroom fittings. The first church in Gothic Proper was round the corner, in Broughton Street, Gillespie Graham's Catholic Chapel of 1813, now St. Mary's Cathedral and much altered. It was a modest effort, for the Catholics were a poor body. Almost immediately afterwards, and again in York Place, a more costly work was begun in St. Paul's Episcopal Church. Archibald Elliot was the architect and English Perpendicular was his model. The Gothic Revival was so little a revival and so much a fashion book style that many years passed before its Scottish practitioners actually went to the native Gothic for their sources, which gives the older work a strangely exotic appearance. Playfair laced

92   Masons at work on the Scott Monument

93   A group of Newhaven fishwives

From photographs by D. O. Hill, c. 1845

94 Interior of the Quadrangle of Heriot's Hospital

his Italianate church of St. Stephen with awkward hints of Gothic. It is an extraordinarily gawky building, thanks to the spite of the Town Council which ordained that it must obstruct the view of the Edinburgh Academy behind. The Academy had been founded by Scott, Cockburn, and others who had cordially hated their school-days at the City's High School and considered its education inept. They started the Academy to provide a sound classical education : anticipating that, lacking endowment and having to charge higher fees, it was likely to be more select forbye, and that its institution would enrage the City authorities. Their petty revenge is a pity, for the modest Academy would have formed a much better termination to the slope from Frederick Street. It is one of William Burn's best works, probably because funds were not lavish and few frills could be afforded. It contrasts very favourably with his ponderous work at John Watson's School at Belford. John Watson's is not to be confused with the more renowned George Watson's, now housed at Myreside but formerly in a pleasant classical building by the Meadows at Lauriston that had originally been the Merchant Maidens' Hospital.

These schools and hospitals were a favourite endowment of Edinburgh merchants. The first of them, and by far the most interesting architecturally, is George Heriot's, founded by the goldsmith and banker of James VI. Heriot's (95) is a grand building of the seventeenth century, flamboyantly decorated, and built around a quadrangle (94) that has something of an Oxford College about it—or indeed of the College that Glasgow so foolishly destroyed. It has been changed little, save by the refacing, with stone from the Ravelston Quarry that unfortunately discolours, of the sides and back. The proper front is, of course, to the Grassmarket. At the back Playfair added a little gateway, an amusing pastiche on the old building. Indeed the lavish endowment of Heriot's, well managed by the Town Council, has done much for schools throughout the City : both George Watson's and the Academy feued their land from Heriot's : and in various places are to be found, in progressive decadence, school structures " in the style of Heriot's," the trademark of the Trustees.

After William Burn came David Bryce, and with him Scottish architecture plumbed the depths of meaningless ostentation, derivation in which every source is arrogantly misunderstood. Most of Bryce's work was done at country seats, where he ruined many a fine old castle, and not infrequently its fine old family as well. However, in 1868–70 he reconstructed the Bank of Scotland on its prominent site at the top of the Mound. The windows notably were glaring and bad when Richard Crichton had built it sixty years before : when Bryce had finished with it everything about it was bad, and it remains to this day a hideous conglomeration of architectural fatuity.

The constancy of the decline in architecture is well illustrated by four hospitals or schools on the north-west of the City. The new Orphan Hospital of Thomas Hamilton built in 1833 is remarkably pleasing with its curious flying-buttressed open towers concealing chimney stacks. Donaldson's Hospital, started in 1842, by Playfair, although rather silly is friendly and inoffensive, and has quality to its detail and a lightness to its ogival towers. Daniel Stewart's, started in 1849, by David Rhind, will do at a distance, chiefly for a gaiety about its almost-onion towers. In 1863 Bryce started the building of the last and most costly of the great endowed schools of Edinburgh, Fettes College. It would seem as though the whole art of architecture had dwindled away, quietly, surreptitiously, and then, suddenly, Bryce stood forth, neither naked nor ashamed but terribly top-hatted and heavily whiskered, incapable of learning or digesting, of modesty or misgiving. Fettes College puts his Bank and his Royal Infirmary in the shade. It is a monumental Victorian whatnot, a vast blight and blot looming over a wide area of low country.

v

One of the pleasantest steeples of the New Town is further remarkable in being the work of an amateur. Major Andrew Fraser of the Engineers, who lived nearby in George Street, designed the dainty classical steeple for the oval church of St. Andrew in 1787. He maintained his amateur status by declining any fee for his work. The church itself is remarkable as the scene of the Disruption of the Church of Scotland in 1843, the most spectacular event of nineteenth-century Scottish history, although one of which the importance has notably dwined away.

The operative cause of the breakaway of the Free from the Established Kirk was the question of patronage, the nomination of ministers to livings by heritors. But although this focussed the differences in the Erastian issue, there were others. They arose with the growth of an Evangelical party in opposition to the Moderates, those who maintained the religious tepidity which had replaced the despairing puritanism of the earlier eighteenth century. To some degree the Evangelicals corresponded to the

94

95 The front, formerly the back, of Heriot's Hospital. In the foreground is Playfair's Gateway

96. 97 The front of Caroline
Park, and a detail of the ironwork on the stairs

Oxford Movement in England, and were a wholesome development of conscientiousness. Nor is it just to contrast the English wisdom in avoiding a split with the tragedy of disruption that befel Scotland. Patronage had been reintroduced after the Union. The split could certainly have been avoided had Government consented to settle the differences. But Westminster doggedly denied all demands made upon it : the English members refusing to pay attention to what they considered a merely local and trivial matter. No Government in Edinburgh could conceivably have ignored an issue that gradually became as acute as did that of patronage during the beginning of the nineteenth century. When, in 1929, the two parts of the Kirk reunited, the " Free " element had gained all its points, patronage had long gone, but so, unfortunately, had the fervour and enthusiasm that could have been so much better spent on other things than sectarianism.

For long, of course, the Evangelicals had great difficulty in getting livings from the patrons whose position they disputed. They first gained vantage in the towns, and particularly through the help of the Edinburgh City Fathers. This was through no zeal, but simply that, since the Civic authorities then built and owned all the churches within their jurisdiction and were dependent for their financing upon pew rents, Edinburgh having spent lavishly upon its churches was driven to instal those ministers who could best fill the pews. Andrew Thomson, the first notable evangelical preacher to be brought to Edinburgh, was able to bring the City £1800 a year from rents.

Cockburn and his friends supported the Evangelicals. In 1843 a split appeared inevitable. But what was remarkable, and surprised everyone, was that four hundred and seventy ministers made the *démarche* from the meeting of the Assembly in St. Andrews Church. In doing so they gave up their whole livelihoods and showed themselves prepared to sacrifice everything for principle. The outcome was almost equally impressive. Within a few months, public subscription had raised funds for new kirks, manses, and stipends for all the dissentients : even to the building and endowing of three colleges (the Edinburgh one being the Tudor Gothic building of Playfair that replaced Mary of Guise's house on the Mound). Voluntary subscription gave the Free Kirk an almost equal status with the Established. It was impressive, but it was a misfortune. It weakened the peaceful penetration of a more conscientious attitude to their faith that had been proceeding in the Kirk during the foregoing decade. By unnecessary duplication and by sectarianism it weakened the life of the parishes. The early zeal gave place to a narrow outlook insufficiently balanced by any other, until the Free Kirk became the stronghold of some of the worst exploiters of labour of the Victorian era, although its first Moderator, Dr. Chalmers, had been a trenchant pioneer in the cause of the poor. Lack of established responsibility led the Free Kirk into unfortunate adventures in anti-papistry. The first of these started in 1848, as a counter-blast to the refugees from the famines in Ireland, with the setting-up of the Gayfield Square Mission under a plausible rogue from Antrim, the Rev. Patrick McMenemy : a discreditable campaign that lasted seven years, until McMenemy was had up for resisting arrest in a Liverpool brothel. It had its successors, and the last of them is quite fresh in the City's memory. It may be added that Free Kirk Gothick is consistently a degree worse than Late Auld Kirk Gothick. The most notable aesthetic achievement to the credit of the Free Kirk lies in its having been the cause of David Octavius Hill turning to the camera : which he did originally to take photographs of members of the first Free Assembly as cartoons for a very bad all-in painting.

Modern Times

I

THE DISRUPTION SET THE STAGE FOR THE VICTORIAN AGE IN Scotland. The year before, Queen Victoria had paid her first visit, continuing the process of the Rediscovery of Scotland by the Royal Family that had been inaugurated with such pantomime splendour by George IV. The '45 was forgiven, its significance forgotten and only the romance cherished. With brilliant feminine inconsistency and discrimination Queen Victoria professed herself a Jacobite. Scotland, to whom so many outlets had been denied, with the further handicap of a divided Church, settled down to the solemn business of making money, and for half a century succeeded amazingly. So much so that for a time she seemed to be a rival to England. However, England had the Parliament, which, even before the days of authoritarian regime, could prove itself a decisive factor.

The faults of the Victorian Age, and even many of its merits, are not of the most sympathetic. The period when it was the fashion, and perhaps needful, to debunk it, has passed. We may now look at it less impatiently, and to-day feel something of awe before a period so serenely assured and self-confident. Whatever its numerous faults, it must remain in history a Great Age : a tag that, whatever our merits, our own age will certainly not achieve. It may be that all Great Ages have to be paid for, and that our generation is paying the Victorian account : in which case a certain resentment against our recent predecessors is at least understandable.

Edinburgh came out of it pretty well. As the centre of banking and insurance, she was able to prosper without having to indulge speculative industry. Her factories for the most part manu- factured goods of solid worth, not quickly to be superseded : beer and whisky, flour and meal, biscuits, anaesthetics, drugs, yarns. Mostly they were reasonably small, and it is remarkable that the City should have grown so steadily, with acres of well- built houses north to Leith (99, 100) and Newhaven (98), west to Murrayfield, south to Blackford Hill. The built-up area doubled itself between 1850 and 1900 : and if most of the new housing was not beautiful, it was solid and presentable, with none of the cowed monotony of the building of the First Great Uneasy Peace.

Intellectual life was not left to depend upon business success. True, there was little enough that was cogent in literature after Stevenson took his consumptive body abroad, and Carlyle had pontificated his way to Chelsea in his hopeless effort to cure his intellectual presbyopia. The Edinburgh painters of the time were for the most part solid craftsmen, but none of them had the brilliance of Allan Ramsay, the poet's son and exquisite portrait-painter, or Sir Henry Raeburn. More impressive artists have since established themselves : Peploe and, to-day, William Gillies, and the sculptor, Hew Lorimer ; while in architecture, Sir Robert Lorimer's interior of St. Peter's Church is far finer than anything done by his Victorian predecessors. It was in Medicine and Science that Edinburgh shone, and here indeed she made most respectable contributions.

Of all the many great doctors of the time probably Sir James Young Simpson was the giant. His place in Edinburgh had something akin to Scott's. Visitors came from afar to see him, not only for his science, which gained him awards and recognition throughout the world, but for a remarkable personality. He entertained lavishly in his house in Queen Street, lectured, wrote his books, and even some verse, and yet was an indefatigable practitioner with a great reputation for his generosity to the poor. Besides his all-important application of chloroform, his clinical researches and hospital reforms revolutionised healing. He was a man of piety and good companionship, and the most generally popular public figure of his time.

Graham Bell of the telephone and Clerk Maxwell, the discoverer of the wireless ray, were others who kept Edinburgh in the front of the developments of the time. Medical textbooks and scientific treatises came from the Edinburgh presses. Publishing, both of books and of periodicals, flourished better than they do to-day. The *Scotsman* had been founded in 1817. Cockburn heralds it as an innovation in Scottish newspapers. Its predecessors were servile rags over which the *Scotsman* at once established its ascendancy. Although started in the Whig interest, it is now rather Tory in its politics : still privately owned, it retains to this day perhaps a better record of consistent integrity and scrupulous reporting than any other daily paper of as long a history. It has always been reputed rather heavy in character, which is perhaps true, but is a small fault compared with those other faults of its more sparkling contemporaries. To-day the *Scotsman*, the

98   Home of the fisherfolk : a Newhaven close

99   The Shore, Leith

100   The Old Harbour, Leith

Evening News, and the *Evening Dispatch* are the only Edinburgh dailies. Of periodicals, the *Edinburgh Review* died some years since. The venerable *Blackwood's* survives unsullied, as does *Chambers's Journal*. There is an illustrated monthly, the *S.M.T. Magazine*; the *Weekly Scotsman*; and the intelligent *Scots Review*. Apart from Law publications, I think that is all, and it does not seem a complete selection for a Capital.

Edinburgh had her share of the obverse side of the Victorian gold-piece, the squalor and destitution bred of the Industrial Age. Even up to 1914 there was desperate drunkenness, and on a Saturday afternoon the wynds and closes of the Old Town could not safely be penetrated by the polite or squeamish. This promoted the demolition of many of them : not a very intelligent way of remedying an evil. But still there remained much of good-hearted conviviality and lively social life in all walks. There have always been howffs for *Noctes Ambrosianæ* : in fact, approximately on the very site of Ambrose's where Christopher North and the Ettrick Shepherd spent their evenings, there is the excellent establishment of the Café Royal : with its pictorial tiles and sporting stained-glass, its oysters and lobsters and liquors, and crayfish fresh from the Firth.

II

The approaches to the City were very much spoilt during the years 1920–40. Although stone-facing is insisted upon for all new buildings in the central parts, farther out the houses were almost all built of brick or composition stone, either bare or harled with dead-coloured cement mixtures : when it was used, stone was often abused, rendered like an upright crazy pavement. Forgotten were the days when speculative building could achieve the dignity and the unity of the New Town, when houses built to order were also orderly. Even the bad taste was commonly an imported one, to English rural models, making it more strident. Council housing schemes achieved an indescribable grimness and chaos. The vast Niddry Estate of barrack-like flats, plonked down without rhythm or reason, housing ten thousand people without urban amenity, has been a headache for the civic authorities ever since. Slum clearance is so estimable an aim that its promoters are sometimes careless of what they aim it at : and new slums can be worse than many of the old ones. People indiscriminately herded together lose the cameraderie, the social sense and responsibility that they have had even in the poorest quarters. No social uplift can replace the inquiring eye of the kent neighbour. The net result is a regrettable decline in " citizenship." Our forefathers built with stone not from ignorance but because their climate required houses of good bield. The replacing of stone by cavity brick walls to suit manufacturers and unions at the expense of the householder has probably largely accounted for the increase in tuberculosis and other illness amongst tenants moved into new houses from apparently far worse conditions. Altogether, the re-housing of the last peace was for the most part wretchedly misconceived. A great deal of planning theory was evolved as a corrective, but one has yet to be convinced that it will achieve much. In the first place, it has no control over vested interests of capital and labour. In the second, it has its own inherent sillinesses : and less few realistic statements have been made during the last decade than those of some of the more ardent planners. Here, Edinburgh is particularly fortunate in being in the Central and South-Eastern District, since that is under Sir Francis Mears, but its own planning officer will have to prove himself of exceptional wisdom if he is to overcome his initial difficulty of being a stranger to the City. It is typical of the unrealistic nature of the planning panacea that, as though it were some precise science like mathematics, a few degrees and some technical experience should be deemed to qualify a man to re-plan an area with which he has no experience or associations.

Although Edinburgh virtually escaped bomb damage, her housing shortage is grave, and the sensible planning of the area is of acute importance. She is perhaps facing the severest menace to her integrity since the days when she was threatened with being altogether eliminated. The exhaustion, largely due to reckless mining, of the western coalfield makes it seem certain that much of the industry of the Glasgow area will migrate east. Part of Edinburgh herself sits above coal, and much of her immediate environment is rich in coal already earmarked for new workings. There is no evidence whatever that, for all the high-faluting talk, the days of the miners' rows have passed. At this very time so-called temporary houses are being erected for miners : smart at the moment in new paint, but poky and cramped to a degree, and with what would appear to be less insulation from cold and sound than their brick predecessors. (The Ministry of Mines, incidentally, is above any regulations that the Ministry of Health imposes upon everyone else who wishes to build.) Tricked out with modern gadgets and seen as an alternative to mouldering and overcrowded hovels, they have obvious attraction.

101   The City from below Salisbury Crags

102   The Waverley Station at night

104. A horse tram turning out of the North Bridge (1895)

103. The traffic of Princes Street in 1850

But intrinsically they are a menace. They are not houses for civilised people ; they must deteriorate rapidly, and " temporary " is a word that tends to outlive its meaning. It is all very well to speak of the difficulties of the time. Excuses can always be made : no doubt the builders of the miners' rows had excellent ones. The present ideas on housing remain those of a bankrupt civilisation.

Edinburgh may therefore find herself embedded in meanly conceived and disintegrated communities such as would destroy the balance that she has so far successfully maintained. Her eastern and southern approaches may be renowned not for that exciting view of the Castle riding above the grey city, but for an absolute conglomeration of reeking bings. Here again the lack of good faith is evinced. There is no possible justification to-day for throwing the waste from the pits on to the face of the earth. Returned to the disused workings, it prevents the desolating subsidence that cracks up houses and roads and waterlogs farmland. Other countries have long followed this sensible practice, and the only answer responsible authorities will make to suggestions for its adoption here is, " It will put a shilling on the ton ! " As though shilling after shilling had not already gone on to the ton to less good purpose.

Certainly a circumambient mining area is a problem to any city, but its co-ordination and absorption should not be beyond sociological ingenuity. One important asset is a healthy vitality in the neighbouring towns, so that they may not straggle ashamedly towards the bigger burgh, as do Glasgow's neighbours, but constitute vigorous units in themselves. Sir Francis Mears' ring plan for the environs of Dalkeith might well protect the southern approach to Edinburgh from further seedy and slipshod eruptions, and bring again an " organic " life to Dalkeith, itself a respectably ancient and defined burgh. Haddington, Linlithgow, and Peebles, in their different ways could be preserved from the drain towards the Capital that has already seriously afflicted the two former county towns, and reconstituted as central units. Her neighbours and Edinburgh need protection from one another if she is to be saved from macropolitan excess, and they not to be left desolate.

Craigmillar Castle (108) still stands grandly isolated, despite incipient encroachment, a lovely sight and an emblem of our strange history. On the Little France side there are already a couple of bings above the derelict, but still gracious, House of Woolmet, and there seems to be a certainty of " development " across those accessible and singularly attractive fields and farmlands. No amount of community centres and hygienic sinks can of themselves make such development admirable or wholesome. Although at present just across the City bounds, they inevitably focus upon Edinburgh : they have no other burgh adjacent, as have the developments near Musselburgh—that charming township which has so well maintained its individuality that even a tramline link with Edinburgh has not destroyed it. Somehow such developments must be integrated with the City, and somehow they must be kept in check if, passing the half million mark, Edinburgh is not to suffer from bloating.

We have as yet only had vocal opposition to centralisation. Will the tide turn before Edinburgh is the latest victim ? We can only hope. Decentralise society before the atomic bomb does the job for you, might be a cogent slogan, if rather misleadingly negative. Luckily, by the time the recent Report of the Advisory Committee on the City's Development was prepared, the satellite town, and some other concealed evasions of decentralisation had been discredited, clarifying the essential issue as between the inter-relationship of manageable units and the ghastly merging of society into unwieldy masses on the Progressive Highway to Totalitarianism. The Report is perhaps as intelligent a document as could have been produced compatible with prevailing trends. It may be, however, that nothing but a project of revolutionary illumination and conviction would have been of any significance.

At present Edinburgh is an uncommonly pleasant city. She is intimately happed by the country, and her own area is sweetened with many green spaces. The dusty grass of Princes Street Gardens is worn with the feet and bodies of those who slip away from the streets to stroll, or loll, and breathe. Boys play and shout in the Meadows, and old men putt on Bruntsfield Links. The tree-graced undulations of Queen Street Gardens bring repose to the top of the headlong slope to the north. Arthur's Seat (13) rears its handsome height above the King's Park, a brisk climb for the active, with a carriage-way from which the indolent may gain a half measure of the view. Down below it, in still rustic setting, Prestonfield (84) is a most gracious mansion. Bruce's curly gables show pale against the warm colour of the hill. The rooms are panelled and tapestried and painted, with robustest plaster grotesqueries, and Spanish leather stamped and gilded. It is one of the best of that considerable number of ancient mansions that still survive as particular pleasures within the spreading city. They range from the fifteenth century Tower of Liberton, high on the first ridge of the Braid Hills, to such eighteenth century villas as Beechwood at Murrayfield, and such modest mansionettes of the early nineteenth century as

105 The Pentland Hills : Newington in the foreground

106   Peffermill, near Duddingston

107   Lauriston, home of John Law

108   Craigmillar Castle

109   Part of the rock garden, Royal Botanical Garden

110   A George Street shop front

111   A Rose Street pub

Heriot's Hill and Hawkhill to the north-east. Quite a number are of that most delightful of Scottish building styles, the transitional castellated of the seventeenth century such as Pilrig, Peffermill (106), Liberton House, and the Inch. Lauriston Castle (107), the house of John Law, that pioneer financial wizard, is a fine tower, with a breathtaking Victorian addition. It and its grounds are the property of the City and open to the public. The Victorian furnishings and decorations have very sensibly been retained, and will become increasingly interesting as so many other collections of that preposterous phase of interiors are dispersed. Not far away is Caroline Park (96) in its shrinking oasis amongst the Council terrors of Granton ; business premises now, but treated with great respect for its courtly and ogival grandeur and its splendidly vigorous Scottish ironwork. Nearby again, Drylaw is another good house with ironwork of the same tradition. On the western boundary Gogar House is an excellent piece of late castellation. Merchiston Castle has recently had its additions demolished and shows forth now with something of its sixteenth century loftiness. Its parapet was the cogitation parade of that amiable Scottish eccentric, John Napier, the inventor of logarithms. Niddrie Marischal is somewhat heavily encrusted in its additions. The Hermitage of Braid is another house in the possession of the City, and with its singularly deep wooded dell and its modestly Strawberry-Hill mansion, has the eighteenth century arboreal unreality so well suggested by its name.

I have remarked upon the surprising sense of inadequacy that the Water of Leith gives, seen as the watercourse of a great city. It comes into Edinburgh by chance, having had nothing to do with the foundation of the City and only being incorporated late in its history. It is a burn, in fact, a trickle of hill water running twenty miles from its source in the Pentland Hills to the harbour of Leith. It is even sometimes disrespectfully referred to as the Puddocky Burn by the small boys who splash and paddle in its shallows by Canonmills, and catch reidbreisters and mennans, and the trout fry occasionally put down in the water by an optimistic Corporation. In the old days it must have been, for its size, one of the busiest waters in the world. Along less than twenty miles there were seventy mills : in places so close together that there was only a six-inch fall between one lade and the next. Wheat-flour and oatmeal were milled for the provision of Edinburgh, and latterly snuff-milling was quite an important ploy. The last of Leith Water's snuff mills was closed down during the late war on the death of its jolly miller, the worthy Mr. Walker who played on his fiddle while the wheels turned and pulverised the tobacco leaves. There are still a few mills, and the Water sluices a tannery at the Dean, and does some other menial tasks as it passes through Edinburgh.

It enters the bounds at Juniper Green, flowing pleasantly by Colinton and coming to the sterner outskirts of the City at Slateford and Saughton, where the old mansion of Stenhouse Mill is almost the only survivor of more graceful building. At Roseburn it passes near another attractive old house, and then, running under Coltbridge, it succeeds in slipping modestly away from public view, taking a strangely rustic course through banks of grass and willow herb, sleek mallard placid on its surface, and reappears to turn two wheels at Bells Mills, grinding sawdust into a fine powder for industrial purposes. Beyond Belford Bridge the Village of Dean (112) has been an enchanting place; it retains some of its old houses, its lovely little semicircular bridge, and a good deal of its charm. Downstream, the Dean Bridge soars across the old village. It was designed by Thomas Telford to make an imposing approach to the New Town houses on the far bank. It forms a striking viaduct, over a hundred feet above the bed of the little stream, and makes a pleasant conceit of the difficulty of spanning it. The four arches carry over a hundred yards of roadway, the parapets now heightened to discourage suicide. There is something enjoyable about walking across it, especially at night, with such space on either side. Perhaps there are conduits beneath the pavements, for they give an answering echo to one's footsteps, suggestive of the depth below. Underneath runs a red footpath between the bank and the wooded gardens of Moray Place, and passing the mineral spring with its graceful Grecian temple (41) and figure of Hygeia presiding contentedly over the sulphurous waters. The far bank is occupied by the Dean Gardens, with their terraces, lawns, and trees, a great pram parade and a rare place for the games of small children.

From here the Water runs beneath Stockbridge, where in winter its surface is sometimes covered over with a yellowish crust of maculate urban ice, and then curves north by unexpected tracks and garden-ends to the Harbour of Leith and the Firth of Forth.

Edinburgh boasts two large open spaces of an instructive nature : the Zoological Gardens at Corstorphine and the Botanic Garden at Inverleith (109). Corstorphine Hill is a grand site, and well laid out. Its rock provides a pleasant kind of playocky realism for the dens of lions and tigers. It looks out over the City and the village, now suburb, of Corstorphine, which retains of

112 The Dean and the Water of Leith

114 The little seventeenth-century steeple of St. Ninian in Leith

113 The mediæval church of Corstorphine

its past a fat bee-skep doocot and a grand piece of Scottish Gothic in the little stone-roofed kirk (113).   Botany, however, is more easily adapted to a garden than is Zoology, and the Botanic Garden is one of Edinburgh's most delightful amenities.   They are the direct descendant, on the third site, of the seventeenth century Physick Garden, coming to Inverleith from the Nor' Loch bank by way of Leith Street.   In the former policies of the pleasant old house of Inverleith the uneven ground excellently displays the trees and flowering shrubs : walks are high, commanding a panorama of the City, or low and secluded between slopes of grass and foliage, not a house visible.   Here in their season flower lilacs with many shades of variation of sweet smells, and aphrodisiac magnolias : rhododendrons and scented azaleas blaze their hot colours.   The rockery (109) is a maze of great variety, and the hothouses spread a sucking sleepiness around their palms and sinister orchids.   At all times of year, the Garden is a retreat from which one never returns without feeling the better.

Golf courses make for many fine stretches of open green within the City marches.   The Duddingston Course is in the policies of the William Chambers mansion whose lovely gateposts bring such a dramatic break to a line of crawling bungalows.   Duddingston is a most pleasant excursion for a summer evening, so easily and pleasantly reached by the green road from Holyrood, under the Arthur's Seat landmarks, the Gutted Haddie, and Samson's Ribs, and through the Windy Goule.   Duddingston Loch with its many waterfowl and its reed beds and the part-Norman kirk on its bank, proffers wonderful misty evening effects.   And nearby, the Sheep's Heid provides refreshment to the echo of its skittle alley.

There are the green handkerchiefs where bowlers play, and the arenas of football fields of which the biggest is Murrayfield, where in my youth I used ceremoniously to watch the international rugby matches.

IV

I have in a sense known Edinburgh ever since I have known anything, for I was born there in a Victorian villa in the Merchiston airt.   I might almost claim a pre-natal acquaintanceship, for my forebears for many generations made their lives and livelihood in the Capital.   Their names bob up in the old street directories : moving into a house in Princes Street now unrecognisable behind a frontage of chain-store Gothic, into George Street, and farther afield to Gillespie Graham's new desirable residences in Albyn Place. For long a branch of the family had one of the George Square houses, where my grandparents were married. It is now part of the Dominican friary. I stayed for some time as a boy with a grandmother who lived on the heights of Randolph Cliff. In the summer my elder brother and I went hardily to the Drumsheugh Baths to bathe before breakfast and the school we attended near Haymarket. Thither, our walk took us through the New Town streets, round by Glencairn Crescent which we nicknamed Cold Street because in winter the snow lay there longest. I learnt to skate at the Haymarket indoor rink, and put my accomplishment to more exciting pleasure on the creaking ice of the old canal and of casual waters beyond the City. At Randolph Cliff we had that tremendous vista down the Water of Leith to the Forth. We used to make cliff-climbing expeditions, or walk along the roof-tops to stand in the little archway under the last chimney stack, looking down on the traffic crossing the Dean Bridge. Much of the traffic was horse-drawn in those days, and I awoke to the sound of the early morning drays rumbling over the granite sets.

Then there were days of late adolescence masquerading as young manhood : the grand balls in the eighteenth century ballroom of the Assembly Rooms, its great mirrors reflecting the glitter of our animation. By present standards the suppers were incredibly lavish, indeed, though, by any standard they were excellently done—turkey and game, lobster and salmon, caviare and pâté, meringues and fruit salads and inexhaustible champagne, and at about six in the morning the brusque stimulus of bones and bacon and beer.

I sat for two sessions in a lecture room of the Old Quad, failing matriculation. But I took far better from the University than any degree, or any days of alma-materdom, stealing my wife from her first-year studies. There were evenings catching the Orkney boat at Leith, with admirable fish teas at the Peacock in Newhaven before it was redecorated beyond recognition. We walked and talked through Old Town and New and along the Water of Leith, drank our coffee in an Italian café with an upper chamber looking out on St. Giles, and had meals in the genial atmosphere of the Chinese Restaurant in Chambers Street. We were married in the stiff little classical kirk of St. Bernard, and lived *almost* in Saxe-Coburg Place for a little while. Mostly, we lived outside Edinburgh, coming in for parties and celebrations and what one delighted to call business.

My young brother came up in his lum hat from Fettes, with a staggering appetite for all kinds of indigestibles to be assuaged at the excellent pastrycooks of Princes Street. He was a mountaineer, ettling to be an airman, and he had climbed by moonlight all over the monstrous roofline of Fettes.

Perhaps, altogether, I know Edinburgh too well to have experience of the unfriendliness and starchiness of which she is sometimes accused. The hardest thing I know of her is that dry deathly east wind which, despite popular belief, is not the prevailing wind, which comes from the west, but is certainly the most formidable element of a climate that generally is dry and wholesome. Often in summer there are haars, blown in from the sea, but the atmosphere in spring and autumn is quite singularly clear and translucent, making for a beautiful visibility.

There is, I think, one thing that may give rise to an illusory lack of hospitality and forthcoming on the part of the Edinburgher. I would define it by a contrast between the Theatre and the Cinema. One is surprised if one has for long only visited the cinema to find, on revisiting a theatre, how much greater a demand is made upon one by the living stage. The spectator has to bring something to it if he is to get anything from it. So with Edinburgh. I think those who find her unrewarding have grown too used to a cinema atmosphere of town life—an atmosphere in which amusement and entertainment thrust themselves upon one just as the vast recorded voices and massive close-ups of the film engulf the spectator. He who comes to Edinburgh has to bring his own responsiveness, and then I think he will rarely be disappointed.

Edinburgh still maintains her tradition of a tolerance that is really a warm affection for eccentrics, so long as their eccentricity springs from the heart. She is perhaps impatient of those to whom eccentricity is an intellectual make-up. Large enough to sustain a stimulating variety of life, she is not so large that her citizens suffer from a perturbing loss of identity such as in some places seems to inspire a shrill minority to self-establishment by the painful flimsy of self-advertisement.

Certainly, there are grave lacunae in her repertoire. Although she has good theatres, importing excellent actors and the gamut of London plays, there has yet to be an Edinburgh Theatre, creative, and interpretative of the life of the nation. The magnet of London centralisation drags away too many of the abler young men who might enrich her life. It becomes an effort and an act of self-denial and impoverishment to stay, and asks too much of many. I think I never felt the beheadedness of our Capital so much as on Victory Day, 1945. The crowds could only mill in circles. Holyrood was closed and shuttered : the Castle the utility lodging of a guard, with a small military hospital. No one could have thought of mafficking outside that emblem of an empty administration, impotent of decision, obedient to the whistle of senior civil servants in Whitehall—St. Andrews House. The awful fact was that there was no living symbol of Scotland before whom the people of her Capital could express their rejoicing, nobody to personify our country. I believe the American Red Cross in Princes Street became the focus, where the G.I.s distributed cigarettes and gum to the wandered crowd.

In the end, the future of Edinburgh must, very properly, lie with the future of the country of which she is the Capital. Despite Glasgow and despite the limitations on her leadership, she is emphatically the First City in the land. One is reminded of that again and again. From Edinburgh one can see Lowlands and Highlands and the intimate inroad of the Scottish sea. The City bounds themselves enfold moorland, a hill of sixteen hundred feet, and even a sea island of the Firth. Wherever I have lived— in the Border Country, in the Province of Galloway, in the Highlands under the Monadhliaths, in these incredible independent islands of the West—I have always felt the country's strong-forged ties with its stately Capital.

Index

(The *numerals in italics* denote the figure numbers of illustrations)

109

INDEX

INDEX

INDEX

The North Prospect
of the City of Edenburgh

PROSPECT OF H